Prayer of the Heart

By
Reverend
Carol Ruth Knox, Ph.D.

Coy F. Cross II, Ph.D. Editor

Koho
Pono

Koho Pono, LLC

Prayer of the Heart

First Paperback Edition 24June2016

ISBN: 978-1-938282-18-8 (trade paper)
ISBN: 978-1-938282-19-5 (ebook)

"Carol Ruth Knox was an insightful and inspiring spiritual visionary. This is a treasure trove on her finest work."

- Rev. David McArthur, J.D., Senior Minister, Unity of Walnut Creek

I first found Unity in 1972. Rev. Carol Ruth Knox was the minister and I was attracted immediately to her positive, life-affirming message. She was out on the edge, ahead of the times, and I loved her weaving of Quantum Physics with spirituality.

- Rev. Cindy B. Wright

"I loved Carol's teachings... I was immediately drawn to them from the first time that I heard and read them. She was the beginning of my knowing that I also was a mystic."

- Dr. Marj Britt, Senior Minister, Unity of Tustin

"As a Unity Minister of 27 years and a psychotherapist of 35, I have met 100s of teachers whose teachings have influenced me. However, only a few remain in an inner circle of influence and they are always with me and guiding me along the way: Rev. Carol Ruth Knox is one of these people."

- Rev. Suzanne Carter, M.A., L.P.C., Unity Minister, 1986

"I had the good fortune to have studied with Dr Carol Ruth Knox just after she finished her dissertation on the Prayer of the Heart. What astonishing work and [it is] far ahead of its time, even though [it is] based on an ancient prayer practice.

Kudos to Coy for preserving this most important piece of spiritual work for us, and for bringing it forward from the silence of the archives! We are blessed."

> - *Deborah Heartwood, MA, Senior Prayer Chaplain, Unity Churches*

"Carol Ruth Knox will take you from the mundane to the metaphysical as you read her words. She was a spiritually gifted teacher who used her own growth as stepping stones to teach the path of God. She was a mentor and great friend whose love of life was shared by all. I loved her deeply."

> - *Jo Coudray, Member, Unity of Walnut Creek*

"Since reading, listening and discussing the teachings of Carol Ruth Knox with Coy Cross, I continue to breathe into the prayers of the heart, coming to a song to sing through the pain, coming back to the cycle of love and strength. When stilling myself to match my own heart, as Carol often taught, I also hear, 'God is in this too, I as one of many, can see this differently, have mercy on me, forgiveness is at hand.'"

> - *Debbie Adams*

DEDICATION

I dedicate this book to the Reverend Carol Ruth Knox, my mentor and friend; and to her extended biological and congregational family.

Acknowledgements

In 2013, Unity of Walnut Creek, where Carol Ruth served as minister for 17 years, graciously granted me license for all her material. Later in that year, I edited and published *The Path of God*[i], a compilation of eleven Sunday lessons in 1986. In 2014, *The Incredible Journey*[ii], the second of her books, was published.

I am grateful to: Reverend David McArthur, Senior Minister at Unity of Walnut Creek, and the Center's Board of Directors for granting me the license for this material; Scott Burr and Dayna Hubenthal of Koho Pono Press for their professional help and constant advice and support; my friend Gail Derin for her expert eye in editing, my family for their continued love and support.

---

[i] Carol Ruth Knox, ed. Coy F. Cross II, *The Path of God* (Clackamas OR: Koho Pono, LLC, 2013).

[ii] Carol Ruth Knox, ed. Coy F. Cross II, *The Incredible Journey* (Clackamas OR: Koho Pono, LLC, 2014).

PREFACE

Prayer of the Heart: A Method of Transformation is based on Carol Ruth Knox's doctoral dissertation, a weekend workshop she conducted in October 1986, and Sunday talks she gave on the subject.

Dissertations, by their very nature, are not written for the general public's reading enjoyment. For one thing they are written in the objective, impersonal style required by the academic community. In editing Carol Ruth's dissertation for publication, I have taken the liberty to include parts I consider relevant and to exclude those written merely to meet dissertation requirements.

I have also rewritten the dissertation passages in "first person," excluded long quotations and opinions from "experts" that Carol Ruth used to "prove" her assertions. I choose to let her writing stand on her own authority.

Additionally, I substituted explanations from her workshop and Sunday lessons when I felt these were clearer and more easy to understand.

Although I have extensively edited the original dissertation, my purpose is to make Carol Ruth's teaching more understandable and readable. I have conscientiously endeavored to stay true to her words and meaning.

TABLE OF CONTENTS

FORWARD

*Outside and even within the Church, modern man is...
indifferent to religion as he knows it, and yet his
nervous restlessness, his chronic sense of frustration, his
love of sensationalism as an escape, his fitful use of
every substitute for religion from state worship to
getting drunk, show that his soul still desires that
release from itself, that infusion of life and meaning
through being possessed by a power greater than itself,
which is found perfectly in union with God alone.*

Alan Watts[iii]

Aspiration is essential to human existence. The word aspiration literally means "to breathe towards"; it is an immutable movement within each human being. When one part of the life is complete, the surge of aspiration moves again, leading ever onward towards something new. As more and more aspects of the life are completed and integrated (the physical, personal relationships, achievement, and social involvement), aspiration inclines toward the

---

[iii] Alan Watts, *Behold The Spirit* (New York; Vintage Books, 1972), pp. 3-4.

concept of God, the sense of Oneness. The longing for a Higher Part of existence does not always express itself as religious dogma or rituals.

Aspiration, as an aspect of human existence, is not always conscious. Even though it is intrinsic, it can dwell within, unknown, and never surface except as the result of crisis, "an act of God," or even boredom with life itself.

For example, any encounter with the possibility of nonexistence can be a powerful trigger which causes a person to know this aspiration pushing on his existence. The possibility of nonexistence can be encountered through death of the body or death of the self while living (as in divorce, illness, loss of prestige or money, or powerful life changes). All of these can be powerful triggers.

One can ignore and repress this pull of nonexistence by running away from it into activity, perennially falling in love, losing oneself in insidious depression, idle chatter, work, or endless emotions. Still it is there wanting direct attention.

Aspiration is also reflected in the person who strangely finds himself no longer inclined towards the material world, yet fully seeking to make peace with that world as an expression of God—he/she now directed by the power of aspiration encounters his humanity as an aspect of Divinity.

Once felt and experienced, through whatever medium, the urgings of aspiration move one towards the goal of unification with God. Being unified with God, one experiences the sense of wholeness, harmony and peace in the midst of and in spite of the life conditions. A resounding belief in an unshakable, loving power, God substantiates one's life, actions and meaning. This singular goal, unification with God, can become the aim for one's life. In the language of mystics, saints, religious devotees, and the common person who is profoundly aware of the deeper movements and urgings of his inner life, it is ultimately the only goal.

Alan Watts acknowledges that churches have failed to bring this awareness to humanity.

> *Today, in church and out of church, there are thousands of souls who realize in varying degrees of clarity that what they want from religion is not a collection of doctrinal and ritual symbols, nor a series of moral precepts. They want God himself... they want to be filled with His creative life and power; they want some conscious experience of being at one with Reality itself.*

> *Knowledge of God, the realization of one's union with God, in a word, mysticism, is necessary.*[iv]

An inherent aspiration can fire at any moment, whether through crisis, fear, existential despair, or at the 'hand of God'. That aspiring urge moves us towards a sense of potential union with God. It carries us along. The long range effects can be seen as old parts drop away and new ones, out of an unknown self, appear; only to become the next old to be dropped away. Keeping our attention on God becomes mandatory in order to sustain our life with some thread of continuity as this pruning and reshaping of our personality takes place. The development of courage as well as a willingness to participate in the process with a total awe-inspiring trust is essential.

The intensity of this challenge inspired many people to recognize the need to cluster with others who were doing the same work. Each group had a set of standards and rules which fit their particular belief of how this work needed to be done. For instance, the Essenes built their community around the doctrine of love—love of

---

[iv] Alan Watts, *Behold The Spirit* (New York; Vintage Books, 1972), p. 15.

God, virtue and mankind. The Therapeutae yearned for a deathless and blessed life, since they recognized that having been moved into this new intent for their life, their mortal life had ended. The Pharisees' highest aim was to reach such a state of holiness that they could perform miraculous cures and prophecy; and the Roman Catholic monastics gradually gathered themselves around certain Christian models and goals. Throughout history, it is obvious that having a fellow traveler, with whom one can share the similarity of the process, test out the new territory, and at the same time dare to remain almost alone and fathom one's depths, is a sweet blessing and may be even mandatory.

Many valuable, exciting, workable psychological, transformative and growth oriented systems provide for self-clarification, adjustment, understanding and even occasional peak experiences, all of which are essential in the catharsis and synthesis of a human life. Yet, each appears to miss that added, special ingredient, which the "spiritual" element offers—a higher goal for human aspiration, the power and availability of the Divine spark within, and its obvious, powerful impact in the transformation of human attitude, personality, expression, and social extension.

To ignore and not directly suggest the presence of this flame within the human being is anachronistic. Humanity has evolved too far for any system to ignore the Divine—it is time to join the Divine in the human, the spirit indwelling the practical. Without the avowed, courageous sharing of this portion of humanity, many people are caught repeating patterns to merely cope with life.

Sadly transcendence and unification are put aside, maybe because of their religious implications, and with this denial of rapture with life, billions of silent dissenters are excluded, through never knowing what was missed—yet suspecting they are missing something. And they are—a relationship with their Spiritual Self, the inner flame, beyond personhood, personality, ego or any of their forms.

1: A HUNGERING HEART

The heart is very important to me. It has been a rather shocking experience to discover that until I studied for and wrote my dissertation I had not really known what the heart was. Like a lot of people, I thought the heart had to do with kindness, being gentle and compassionate, and treating people decently. I had committed to that kind of life experience; I set myself up to act out a certain behavior, thinking that was "heart business."

In today's New Thought teachings, we are told we are in the age of the heart, but I am not sure we understand what the "age of the heart" is. I happen to be one who knows what the "heart business" is about, for I have spent the last eight years with my attention in the heart as a way of opening my heart. I would like to share that experience with you.

Indications of a Hungering Heart

Do you ever feel barren? Do you sometimes experience overwhelming feelings of bitterness and bondage? Do you find yourself bickering a lot, feeling bored with life? Do you occasionally feel as if you are inside a cave, the cave feels gray, and you don't know how to get out?

Do you wake sometimes in the morning without feeling zest for life? You may have slept ten hours, but you are not at all renewed; the primary awareness moving through your head is of relationships that have not treated you right, living situations that don't work, a general feeling like a low-grade headache, as a way of being—does that touch you?

You may be married to the "perfect person"; you may have a wonderful job; you may have worked many different systems; tried to think right and even thought "wrong" and even that didn't work. You may have done fifteen different workshops and experienced what you thought were "openings" only to have the "thing" close down on you and then find that you feel even worse because you experienced "a taste of honey" but you didn't know how to keep the honey, so you returned to the same "buzz of consciousness" which is like a drone. Only that drone isn't the great Om of the Hindus; it is just a "'here I am, again" and "I did not break out of the cave."

I think Unity[v] does an excellent job of helping us to feel comfortable with being as we are—that there is nothing wrong with anger; there is nothing wrong with inner hunger; there is nothing wrong with passion or love or lust or jealousy or anxiety.[vi] I think we have been taught really well to trust that part of God's process within ourselves. Yet, the phenomenal perfectness of God's working within us is that God does not leave us alone. And even though we accept our general state of beingness,[vii] there is some urge within that says, "And I know I have a potential for beauty, expression, existence, life, loving, as a way of being in the world, and I am not tapping into it." Right?

We know that we can try to accept ourselves for all we are and yet, there is a stronger urge, a driving power within. The way it works is to keep pushing on the insides of our present state of consciousness. As it pushes, it tends to create greater disparity. Usually we tend to project the disparity upon our relationships, our working

---

[v] Unity, when capitalized, is a non-denominational Christian movement.

[vi] Some Unity ministers might disagree with this statement.

[vii] (Explanation) This means the fullness of all that God is.

situations and our general environment. As we project it onto others, we are actually trying to push out the walls of our consciousness so that we can let in more light, so that we can be touched again by a memory of a potential way of being living within.

Taking part in this expanding process is like living inside an eggshell. The process of life is that once you have completed one state consciousness or existence (an egg), you find that it no longer satisfies you. So there is a push on the edges of that limit. The minute the urge begins and you are able to push your way through, you stretch the sides of the egg to create porous holes whereby you might move through and enter into a whole new space. Once there, you relax and say, "Aah," only to discover that the minute you said "Aah," you become a part of a bigger egg in which you exist causing the pressure mechanism to work its way out again.

Let me remind you that the way the pressure shows itself is through our projections on uncomfortable relationships, financial situations, nagging personalities, or job experiences and anything else we can mention. But the process keeps moving on, changing, stretching.

I believe that our consciousness is saying, "I want to leap from one way of being into another way of being, and I'm looking for a connecting link." The connecting link that I discovered was entering into my heart.

I entered into my heart clearly in March of 1979 after two years devoted to working with the Prayer of the Heart. The day I entered, I knew I had made a shift to another level of transcendence and since that moment I have stayed in that place. Always, of course, wondering whether and when I will be kicked into another level.

I share this with you to make something obvious. A lot of teaching concerning the heart is unclear. I wouldn't believe I had the authority to write about this, until I had devoted eight years of my life to studying and researching the spiritual heart through the great saints and spiritual teachers over the past two thousand years.

We have been confused about what it means to be in the heart. As mentioned earlier, many of us have thought that 'heart' meant coming from niceness and kindness. The truth about studies of the heart, spiritually, is the heart has to do with an energy; it has to do with a flame; it has to do with knowing how to excite that flame, how to stimulate and empower that flame, so that the flame takes over the activity and movement and direction of the life.

Through this activity, the whole system is then incorporated. The flame becomes the purifier, the refiner and the grower of the whole system—so that you give up control and allow it to become the worker and the seeker and the urger. When this is completed, it is as if a flame has been lit in oil and then set onto the water of life.

As the water of life moves up, our usual tendency is to move up with it and as it moves down, so do we. But this flame, once lit, rather than losing oneself in the down and ascending when in the heights, the flame burns slowly and smoothly through the whole experience. This flame has released conditions, duality, terms, and expectations with regard to life. It is a profound state and it is the nature of transcendence.

Transcendence is not killing the lower for the sake of the higher. It is confirming that the transcendent part, the flame in the heart, knows how to ride with the whole process without thinking it should be any way other than the way it is—because the way it is perfect.

How do you touch your heart? Not through the emotions, not through sexuality, not through the primal part (none of which are "bad" or out of order). Then how, when you find yourself fed up with that mid-range of life, how do we move on via the heart?

Well, first you must know that there is a heart waiting within you. There is a heart lying in you hungering and wanting your attention. It often feels left out. You will know it is left out when you find yourself bitching, bickering, banging on your inside head, barricaded. All those symptoms are ever saying is, "Please come find me." It is waiting for you to recognize it and it will spark and you will feel enflamed as you tend to it more and more.

I would like to read to you how the saints who have studied this for over 2,000 years have touched it. The following quotation is from Theophan the Recluse, a Russian monastic, who brought this 2,000-year-old practice to public attention in the late 19th century. Pay attention because this is now your work!

He says, "Feeling towards God—even without words—is a prayer. Guard this gift of feeling, given to you by the mercy of God. *[This is nineteenth century English, so be careful of it.]*

How? First and foremost, by humility, ascribing everything to grace and nothing to yourself. Secondly, dwell in grace and do not turn your heart or thought to anything else except necessity. Be all the time with the Lord. *[And I am pointing to my heart.]* If the inner flame begins to die down a little, immediately hasten to restore its strength *[by bringing the attention into the heart]*."[viii]

My Personal Journey

Let me begin by sharing my personal trip as a woman who has attempted to integrate a big happening in her life. Ten years ago I was catapulted into a powerful spiritual experience, which had no definition, no guidelines, and no maps whatsoever. It affected me so deeply that I had to go looking for something to give meaning to what was happening to me.

Whenever a person goes through trauma or crisis, there has to be a way to put meaning into it, so you can live with yourself for the rest of your life. In my search for meaning, I discovered an age-old

---

[viii] Writings from the *Philokalia, 2ed.* on Prayer of the Heart, trans E. Kadlubovsky and E.H. Palmer (London: Faber and Faber, 1954), pp. 148-149.

monastic tradition, well-oriented in profound spiritual truth, which I would like to share.

At that time, I had completed my doctoral studies, but not my dissertation. I was already a very successful minister. I built the Unity Center in Walnut Creek from 20 people to around 350 at that time. Now it is up over 500 on a Sunday. So I was at the top of the scale.

I had also just recently fallen smashingly in love. For the first time in my life, I had time to really open myself up to love and to be loved in a deeply meaningful way. I had fallen head-over-heels in love.

The previous year, I had sat in a Gnostic mysticism class and gotten quite angry with the teacher because I felt myself slipping out of my basic structural belief system. Very important words: "slipping out of my basic structural belief system." I became terribly scared. He had even questioned the Law of Mind Action.

Do you know the Law of Mind Action? If you have gone to Unity School or taken important Unity classes, you have to reiterate it this way, "Like begets like." Here is another part of it, "What you think you get back." "What you put out to the universe, you will receive," which translates into, "If I am good, I'll get good stuff back. If I am bad, I'll get bad stuff back." A basic, simple, great coming to realize, that this is possible. But he began to force me to question by asking, "Is it always true that the Law of Mind Action always takes place?" Having been a minister for six years at that time, but involved in Unity for 38 years, I was at a tough age to have my structure unraveled. But things weren't working any more.

I'm sure that had something to do with my experience the following year, when I was sitting out in my backyard, in a meditative state. On a Monday afternoon around 12:30, suddenly, from out of nowhere, a very powerful force entered into my state of well-being. I know it is not the Devil. I don't believe in the Devil or evil. But some stupendous force was taking me and breaking me apart. I felt as if I was dragged out my present state of existence into a world of non-definition, where all my limits were taken away and I was scared out of my wits. My sense is that I was moved in an instant into the world in which I now live in. It was so frightening and I had no way to understand it. But I had to someway, somehow put the lid back on it and bring myself down into what I knew. It took me nearly three hours to return to what felt normal.

The important thing about this and what I have learned was that I was on course. Everything I had set my life toward, which was to become a living mystic, was taking place. But I didn't trust the process and my spiritual principles were about to deepen, because I was going to learn to trust everything, including what I would define as absurd stupidity and horror.

For the next year, I was almost continually born, broken, born, broken, born, broken. It was as if "it" would give me a second of peace and then suddenly "it" would break me apart again. If you ask me what "it" is, I don't know. "Is it me?" "Is it something terribly important to me?"

I was being taken out of myself. I had worked hard to develop a powerful ego. What I didn't realize at the time was that that ego was being smashed. My world structure was being taken away. My capacity to control was being eliminated. My ability to take something and follow it through with focus to completion was broken.

I went to a psychiatrist. Luckily the psychiatrist said, "Carol, there is nothing wrong with you psychologically. What is happening to you is spiritual. Keep on the course you are following. Trust it. Get comfortable with it until it completes itself. We are glad this is what is happening to you."

The whole receptive domain was being awakened. Although I had taught people to enter into the receptive domain for years, I didn't know how to hang out there. I knew only how to keep control.

I became terribly depressed. I probably was clinically depressed. I had great difficulty in keeping going. I didn't know why I was getting up in the morning. I lost all sense of meaning. I kept on doing my job. I don't know how, but I did. I kept getting up there and doing my shtick. In other words, enough of me was organized that this could be played out through me. I seriously considered killing myself. I never took any action to do it, but I seriously considered doing that. God had left me and I was alone and lost.

I thought maybe all I needed was rest, maybe I was burned out, maybe I was used up. I went to Hawaii for three months in the summer of 1977. Instead of getting healed, like I thought I would, I didn't get better. With the openness and emptiness in Hawaii, my insides heaved up even greater despair and disconnection, doubt and questioning.

After I came home from Hawaii, I went to my dissertation advisor. She suggested, "Why don't you turn your dissertation into the miracle that is happening to you." Bless her heart! The miracle? This was no miracle. This was Hell. I was dying. I was being eaten up. I was losing it. That is how I felt. I was losing it.

She then put into my hand *The Dark Night of the Soul*[ix] by St. John of the Cross. It is a book that most people, especially in the Unity movement, are afraid of. This is a realm of the spiritual life generally avoided in Unity's writings. When I read it, I found me in these simple words "You will know you are in the Dark Night of the Soul when there are no meditations, no inspirations and no imaginations." As I read that line over and over again, I said, "This is me. This is me." Finally I began to have a sense that maybe I was okay, even though the whole thing looked like I was totally out of order, as if I had blown it.

Until this point my prayer life had been: (and see if you can identify with it) if things weren't going well, I prayed. Rarely did I pray if they were good. If I wanted something badly, I really worked

---

[ix] St. John of the Cross, *The Dark Night of the Soul*, 3rd ed. trans. E. Allison Peers, (New York: Image Books, 1959).

internally. And, I was good at that. I have drawn treasure maps. I have built two churches. I have created crowds. I just realized today that when I went to Brown University to do my masters work that I got a scholarship and I ideated that, I pictured that, I created that.

I knew what conditional prayer was like and I think an awful lot of the world knows what conditional prayer is like. I want you to know that was very important with me. I can remember standing in my new shower I just had built in my home. I would be doing affirmations with all diligence and dedication:

"Let me feel enthusiastic, life-filled, joy-filled."

"Today is a holy day, precious in the light of God."

"I am filled with God's spirit."

And there was big voice inside that said, "Oh, no. You are not. Don't kid yourself."

And, I couldn't kid myself any longer. I don't know if you know that experience, but it is a powerful one. I don't know if you know the affirmation-denial experience: as loud as you say the affirmation there is this little "ghostie" chasing you saying, "No, it isn't so." Do you know what I mean by that?

There is something about that, you see, that has to be addressed in the spiritual life. You can't just keep living like that. That has to be addressed. But what is being addressed?

What is being addressed is that the system, you, a powerful system developed by God, knows certain things about truth and about the depth at which you want to live. So when something inside you says, "This isn't the way it really is. This is a lie to my system." Then something is calling you that says, "How do I live deeper than that or beneath that?" "Deeper than that." Not "above it." Not "beyond it." Not "better than." But, "deeper."

You see, the funny thing is that I couldn't make the Unity principles work anymore. No matter what I did with my brain, I couldn't get positive thinking anymore. I was like a wretched, tarnished soul being dragged through this literal, internal holocaust, being taken into ever deeper, deeper parts of being that I had never known were there.

I read probably 150 works of the great saints throughout Christian and even pre-Christian history. I studied, for instance, the *Philokalia* and

The Art of Prayer[x]. I poured over the words of St. Theresa of Avila, Julian of Norwich, and St. John of the Cross. They all pointed to the same thing: continual prayer.

Several books described *The Prayer of the Heart*, a simple discipline and vehicle through which vast potential for human transformation may be released.

Historically The Prayer's roots may be seen in pre-Christian and Christian Gnosticism and mysticism. It developed in the midst of early Christian doctrinal definitions, yet removed from the main stream in the caves of the earliest monasteries in northern Egypt. By the eleventh century, a treatise attributed to St. Symeon the New Theologian called this method of interior or spiritual prayer, "Hesychasm". The Prayer of the Heart flourished in nineteenth-century Russia and is gaining attention in the West in the mid to late twentieth century.

---

[x] Writings from the *Philokalia, 2ed.* on Prayer of the Heart, trans E. Kadlubovsky and E.H. Palmer (London: Faber and Faber, 1954) and *The Art of Prayer*, ed. Igumen Chariton of Valamo, trans. E. Kadloubovsky and E.M. Palmer (London: Faber and Faber, 1966).

The sense of the Prayer of the Heart is found, of course, in most of the religious traditions (the contemplative tradition of Western Christianity, Sufism, Hasidism, Japa Yoga of the Hindus, various aspects of the Pure Land Buddhism, and Zen Buddhism). My focus is primarily on the Christian prayer; however, I especially focus on the Eastern Orthodoxy and the Greek-Byzantine interpretation.

I have been deeply affected by the Prayer of the Heart. I began carrying the Prayer five years ago, and its process in me has designed and developed this work. The Prayer has become my path; it is all I do now in terms of spiritual inner work. It has altered my personality, allowed me to survive a harrowing personal experience, and comforted me during some most painful physical occurrences. It has clearly influenced changes in my life style, reshaped some of my important religious beliefs, and caused readjustments in many basic attitudes. The Prayer entered my life at the "ripe" time, when I was ready for transformation, and its power pushed me ahead in that process.

Before I committed to the Prayer, I functioned from a strong ego: I knew the sign-posts and operated according to them. Now I am not so sure. Yet that is fine, because ultimately security becomes brittle and narrow, limited and artificial. As I moved along through the days and years, I felt that I had encountered a brick wall and it was it essential that I break through, not with quick blows from sledgehammers, but with the artfulness of living life gently and with love rather than aggression.

In September, 1977, I was offered a road; I took it and it has made all the difference in my life. I feel nothing but gratitude for having taken this step, even though I know the work I have undertaken will never be completed. Seeds of mystical illumination have been sowed in my experience, changing me forever. I am frankly proud of my courage, my willingness to be spun around, and the strength given to me by the Prayer.

2: STAGES OF PRAYER

There is a clear process by which we can unite with the Divine. That process first organizes itself around the Prayer of the Heart which clearly involves four distinct stages. Then as we carry the prayer in our heart, the prayer itself creates its own energy, effects and dynamic. Our ongoing activity of prayer is an experiment in living; one that will never end once begun, and, mysteriously, one which we cannot let go, for in time the prayer takes over our life. Its effect on our total consciousness is an internal process leading automatically from one stage of prayer to the next.

It is important that we recognize the subtlety of this seeking and becoming one with God. Each of us approaches the mind, emotions, and body differently. We can no longer depend upon psychological understanding, being our life's object or instigator, or casting out our humanity and becoming the attitudes and reflections of our past.

Union with God ensures that any physical, mental, emotional disclosure or any external manifestation can only result from internal Spiritual activity and creation. This then becomes our living faith.

Our relationship with life shifts from action to silence, from external motivation to internal beingness, from fear to trust.

There are difficult periods of strangeness and distance from our very life itself, but gradually we gain clarity in the quietness; and our devotion to the prayer moves to the prayer's being our motivation for all thought and action. Surrender becomes our way of life as our understanding grows. Gradually our life moves differently, now from the internal, instead of the external.

The Process

It is apparent that union with God moves into our life either gradually or at some obvious moment. From then on, our life is changed in its direction and intent.

Obviously, not everyone reaches union, even though they may pursue it vigorously and persistently. A person can seek it but not have It take him over.

Also, the experience is not always pleasant. The very nature of this sensitivity, desire, major shift of our life's intention is considered the true activity of God, of God continuing to shape Its unfinished spiritual creation.

Once we move into this point of awareness, we begin to appreciate the necessity of seeking God, of remaining close to God. There is an awe hidden within this awareness—the awe of respect for a mysterious inner force, which when fired and charged works on its own. There is an obvious feeling of losing control, and many people find themselves being pushed, dragged or plummeted into this conscious spiritual life. The awe commands, "Participate, be involved with God, or you cannot go forward, you cannot even survive on earth, for now you are too different." Once we step in or are brought in, the die is cast; only union with God can satisfy.

It is essential, then, that we recognize and honor this Creative Spirit, God, and seek It by participating actively in bringing It more consciously and fully into every moment of our daily life.

Once our soul recognizes its being in God as the source of perfect happiness, then our soul's nature leads us to want to be with this source. Obviously, if we find what truly brings us peace and fulfillment, then we will pursue that with our whole being.

Ordinarily, however, we do not, because our awareness is dim and undeveloped, and what we are seeking is foreign and peculiar to our everyday world. It is not obvious or verbal; it is not clear or explicable; it is mysterious and hidden deep within. But once we discover this source of happiness, It feels like loving our self/Self, and we will pursue it wholeheartedly.

My mother taught me to pray through the Unity movement as I was raised in Unity. No doubt many of you were taught in the same way. I was given very clear guidelines for praying.

When I started praying, it was as an egotist. An egotist prays for God to give them what the person wants. You know that kind of prayer, don't you? That kind of praying is very much supported by positive thinking movements, and by "create your own reality" organizations. Such teachings actually hype you up to make you into a god.

Sometimes I imply that you are a god, but there is a very deep, deep growth that has to occur within us in order to move from thinking you are a god at an ego level, to knowing you are a god from an internal level.

I would assume then, that most of us start out by asking God to give us what we want. If we have an ill body we ask for God to heal it, and God reveals Himself to us when we are healed. If we have depression, then we ask and beseech for it to go away.

Last night when I talked to my mother, she had been listening to Oral Roberts. She said, "Carol, I am at the point where I just want to holler out," because the pain in her system was so deep. Oral Roberts suggests hollering out, beseeching, begging God.

I am putting none of these forms of prayer down, for at times they all work. If we are depressed, we beg to have this thing, this heaviness removed from us. If we have fear, we ask God to take it from us, but we don't understand why God would give it to us. If we feel lack then we ask God to provide us with money. If we don't have somebody to love us then we beg God to provide us somebody to come charging in and fill us with the love force. Well, such prayer <u>does</u> work for a time—it worked in my life for a long time. I hope you have done it enough to know that this kind of prayer works too, but it works for only so long. If you have discovered this, then this material will speak more to you than if you have not.

This kind of prayer starts to fail when all we ask for does not come through. You know about that, don't you—most of those prayers have a 50-50 result factor. Sometimes I think when we are younger the ratio is 60-40 or 80-20 (for), but then a person has a lot more energy for the world and to make things happen and probably does not even understand that is why all is going well. However, once we begin to see that with all our asking, with all our positive thinking, with all our "right" expectations, some things do not come through, then our self-doubt begins to exert itself. Then the movement in our personal consciousness has to seek a different direction.

When this change in awareness started happening to me, I interestingly fell into a very "catholic" position. I read some of the writings of the early Roman Catholic teachers, from the time before it was literally Roman Catholic. During those early years, there was quite a tradition of high prayer. When I sought this new direction and was led to the early Christian teachings, I had to awaken to an entirely new way of relating to myself and to the Universe.

This new way of relating was to understand first that I had not prayed "right". That could sound like a statement of guilt, but it does not feel like guilt to me. It feels like an understanding and a growing awareness of my own Spiritual evolution. I started reading intensely, and as I did, I realized that my life focus had to switch from being external to being internal. I had to move the intention for my life away from the external world's expectations to learning how to relate to my soul at an internal level.

It was through this process that I discovered that there are four stages to prayer, and I would like to share those with you.

I: AFFIRMATION

The first prayer type may be called simply "affirmation". You know it well, especially if you have read a lot of Unity literature. Affirmation is the way that you begin to sow a new thought in your mind, and the new thought is that we have a relationship with Spirit Indwelling.

Once in a class at Unity Center of Walnut Creek, a gentleman raised his hand and said, "What I love is that I am learning a whole new language." It is as if you have grown up with one language and then you go to school to learn a new one. Spiritual awareness is the new language.

To carry his analogy further, as you begin, every word has to be formed very carefully in the mind and in the mouth before it can be spoken. As you do that over and over again, which is the trust process, gradually that moves from the mind down into the heart. So instead of having to give it to yourself from the mind, it is given to you from the heart.

Once the heart takes over, then the mechanism comes to operate on automatic from the inside. In developing one's first stages in prayer, one learns slowly, the new language and attitudes—the concepts and beliefs, and sets them to affirmations.

Thus we begin the process and begin to de-program ourselves from the information of the world, to make the life of Spirit an internal experience where we understand truthfully that all life is a matter of Spirit. Only through affirmations does the message of Spirit, its concepts and values, have the chance to come from an internal space.

There has to be some way for us to experience this long process so the way we start is through affirmations. There is a wonderful story about this process in the book, *The Way of a Pilgrim*.[xi]

II: DENIAL

The second type of prayer is denial. It is equal to affirmation but different. Denial is a tool you can use when you're frightened so the fear will not overwhelm you. That is all.

I don't necessarily care for this type of prayer but it is one of the tools that has been used by mankind, throughout history. Why? Because sometimes, as we all know, you get so frightened that you cannot stand the terror. You know about that. When it hits, then a tool that is available to you is to say, "Get Thee Behind Me, Satan. Just keep away for now. I can't handle you." That is denial. You have the right to do that within yourself. Use it. I have used it tons of times and still do occasionally.

But, as you get stronger, you do not have to use it—you realize that nothing can hurt you. Nothing. Not even your deepest fear.

[xi] *The Way of the Pilgrim* and *The Pilgrim Continues His Way*, trans. R.M. French (New York: Ballantine Books, 1974).

Denial has its weakness, as modern psychology has shown. Denial blocks energy and can leave you without all of yourself, all of your available potential. Denial befits a dualistic philosophy and limits our capacity to accept the entire Universe, to realize that all is God. In seeing these weaknesses in denial, we become aware of a larger potential in human consciousness, which is the third stage of prayer.

III: PRACTICING THE PRESENCE

The first two types of prayer are discriminatory disciplines. Admittedly, they are usually delved into as a means for stabilizing the personality and its relationship to the world.

In the search for inner freedom, many people turn to the religious process. The religious process has a beginning, and with experience and practice the mind and emotions change, the practice works. The inner being becomes refined, and as with any discipline (whether it be sports, developing a relationship, or becoming a professional artist or musician) the subtlety of the internal alteration raises a desire for a closer experience with the goal; in this case, with Oneness. Practicing the Presence is so much closer, easier; one feels more comfortable inside. The externals are not as confusing or threatening. Their power diminishes through the practice.

Peculiarly, the attention to the heart has powerful psychological and physical effects. Psychologically what enters the conscious mind from all the subconscious conditionings does not carry its usual "kick". Physically, nervous tension dissipates and the fear that takes its place has nothing to attach to. The heart remains still and comfortable. Such a tranquilizer does not exist in the material world.

This third type of prayer is the most precious to me. Affirmation and denial are prayer types which are the product and servant of the mind. Yet, we all know that old saying "the mind is the devil's playground". The mind is a place where we believe we exist. The mind is the last threshold to keep us from pure contact with that deep power that is resting in our breasts and chests. The mind is a manipulative thing. It wakes you in the morning with your present problems. It is the thing that talks through you over coffee, that allows you to gossip and prattle on about others. It is that delicious belief in the illusion that anything could be out of order within you.

You know about your mind, don't you? It is that thing that if you add a cup of coffee to it, it hypes up even more. If you take a drag on a cigarette, it moves it along even faster. A nice swig of wine will steady it down and make you think things are okay until the wine wears off and then... there it goes again. It is the thing we all would run away from and I know it well. In order to get beyond the mind, one absolutely must move to the heart. You must move to your heart.

I am going to ask you to do it right now. Keep your eyes open, keep reading, but at the same time, send your attention down into your heart. Notice that almost immediately you must become very quiet.

As you are in your heart, say within, only two words, I AM. Notice that the mind still goes on, but a different energy begins to be created. Are you aware of that? Can you feel it? It is a different energy.

This activity, the Prayer of the Heart, not only elevates consciousness, calms one's being, but it is also a grounding device. Physiologically it is a centering device. It affects the body. Can you feel it? This is called the Prayer of the Heart. This is deeper than affirmation.

If, when you are down inside yourself, you keep your thoughts contained and don't allow yourself to run away into your mental spaces—don't allow yourself to run away into your emotional spaces although they are a whole lot more powerful— something wonderful begins to happen.

The language, the new language, begins to move from being just a mind trip to becoming a heart trip. It becomes so much deeper that this I AM space, whatever it is and no one knows. It begins to talk for you, through you—as if you heard yourself—a channel for the Living Spirit within. Your thought now is no longer of the world—it has transformed into another level. The language of Spirit begins to move in you automatically. Your thought becomes the Christ Spirit speaking through you.

Every morning when I awake now, I go and sit somewhere. I go into this place within me, this I AM, this Kingdom of Heaven within. It has been in the process of being trained now for nearly four years, and I listen and I ask it to speak through me. It has a very pure statement. It says things like, "I am here with you always—trust me—I love you—I care for you—I am protecting you—I will lead you on (and incidentally, I am listening to it now)—I will guide you—I will tell you what next to say—I am the healer—that is all."

It takes tremendous trust to live from this place. A whole new energy is born, and it is not dynamic, exciting, emotional, exquisite, dancing energy. It does not especially care to talk to people. It does not especially care to go to movies. It does not really care about organizations anymore. It does not want to be hassled by the head. It only wants to pray with others through the heart. It would rather be with a flower than a textbook. It would rather be with an animal than a business letter. It would rather listen to the creative voice of Spirit than write it in a book. It would rather heal than chatter.

This practice is so powerful, so essential to our beginnings. This is how we become living monastics—this is how we become convent nuns—but monastics/nuns in the world. We want to make a society where we are living the Spirit wherever we go, where we know that the person who is working the press is carrying the prayer in his heart—where the person who is running our business is carrying the prayer in his heart—where the person who is filling out the stock orders is carrying the prayer in his heart—where we know that the person who is cultivating his garden is carrying the prayer in his heart. When we all carry the prayer in our heart, we will be truly converted and truly committed, and we will not have the need for drink or the need for drugs or the need for alleviation from our own selves.

There can be no higher message than this on what do we do to build a spiritual life. This is not just Carol Knox's message; this message has been with us for as long as man has been on the earth. And, this is what you do if you want to live the life of a spiritual being.

Probably only someone who has a true sense of human potential and their capacity to tap into their real Christ nature can live as the Spring of God. If you believe that you can live as a Spring of God, a fount of God Life—if you believe that, then this is the path you must take. There is no other path for you. This path leaves psychology, sociology, government, medicine behind and goes down a single road, the straight and narrow road, the direct shot to make contact.

IV: GRACE

As with so many experiences in life, there is a moment in which effort, discipline, and practice click into an automatic movement. So it is with prayer. When prayer becomes continuous, then spiritual prayer begins. At this point the fourth type of prayer, the fourth stage of prayer, begins to live within the devotee.

Such activity is a precious moment; this is the cherished goal. Now the human is out of the way, and Spirit lives the being. Now will and ego have so given themselves over to Oneness and our sense is of God living through us. The conversion is completed; our life is being lived through. As Jesus said, "The works that I do in my Father's name, they bear witness to me."[xii]

This experience is grace, so often referred to in the Christian heritage, and so little understood. Many people have gone to ministers, priests, church leaders, begging to know why God does not answer prayer. Often the word has returned, "...have faith... trust." In agony, people have left their churches thinking the teachings dull and stupid, considering worldly knowledge to be far more convincing. What they haven't realized is that faith and trust are the effect of a refined process of inner work, entitled prayer. Faith and trust are a gift, a sense, which was always present. Through our involvement and investment the gift is opened, the sense is allowed to infiltrate our life. Grace is understood as an experience; grace is the keen awareness that Spirit lives in all; Spirit is God.

[xii] John 10:25, Revised Standard Edition of the Bible.

Are there words to describe a matter of timing so subtle, other than to assign this movement from one stage into another as His will, His special grace?

In other words, no one knows the how, the why, or the when of the special "click". Who knows when timing the shift of gears on a car will become an automatic feeling? Who knows when typing will move from conscious thought to freedom without structure? Who knows when our feelings for another will move from liking to loving? It is a matter of timing; it is some "other" factor which nobody can grasp; it is extremely individual, not capable of being judged by variables or other people's wisdom and counsel. So it is with prayer: keep on, practice. At some point we will shift to being moved by Spirit rather than moving Spirit; then we will experience Grace and life becomes a dance.

At times the flow will slow down, shut off, ebb, but now we know to trust, allowing Grace to return quickly.

In this fourth type of prayer, we obviously feel joy, arrival, freedom, relief. It is important to note that our life goes on in this state of awareness and experience. Often the state of Grace does not remain, but now it is near and we can rely on its return. Even if our life becomes threatening, as we grow in understanding, Grace can become nearly constant.

With it also comes the gift of Spiritual prayer: prayer which obviously comes from some part other than mind or emotions. Such prayer is clearly different from asking for ourselves or another; it does not arise from our ego or will. It feels like thought born from Spirit.

It is light, universal, oriented towards serving, not for our self-gain, but as an activity of Spirit.

It is clearly propelled from a higher realm of thought.

Its growing presence alters our usual thought content.

It tends towards giving.

It tends towards more quiet.

It tends towards inner space beyond reflection, words, and thinking. We become prayer itself.

3: THE HISTORY OF THE PRAYER OF THE HEART

By 'the care of the heart,' by becoming detached from all created things, losing consciousness of himself and being wholly absorbed in the contemplation of God, a man could take the leap into the infinite, passing altogether beyond the world of the divine image. At the end of the road was God, and man had only to hurl himself along the road of prayer to see God's face.[xiii]

- Gregory of Palmas

Ten thousand years ago in India and two thousand years ago in Christianity, the little 'pearl' I am going to give to you was shared only with a select few. It was shared with monastics and hermits living in caves—only shared with those individuals totally devoted and committed to loving God.

Why? Because its power and potential is so dumfounding that it was believed that common

---

[xiii] Robert Payne, *The Holy Fire* (New York: St. Vladimir's Seminary Press, 1980), p. 269.

people could not handle it. I don't accept that premise.

The little 'pearl' is this: they discovered that if they brought their attention down into their heart and maintained there, along with a simple prayer that had Universal content and spiritual intent, something profound happened within the being: He/she was transformed, elevated. The cell structure altered, the thought content changed from within, the being evolved.

Let me reiterate. It was discovered ten thousand years ago and usually hidden from the masses, that if one brought the attention into the heart, which is the central organ in the body, that one was transformed.

You see, the heart is vitally important in this. In the chakra system, the lowest chakra is at the base of the spine. The next ones follow the sexual organs, the solar plexus, the heart, the throat, the third eye, and the crown chakra (seven in all). Where does transformation happen? At the heart level.

It all fits, and yet we don't know why it happens. But we do know that if we bring our attention through the mind, into the heart, and wrap it around a simple prayer that is both universal in content and God-centered in intent we are automatically altered, transformed. Even the cellular structure changes and gradually our whole personality and systems evolve into a higher level of expression.

Theologically, the origins of the Prayer of the Heart raise important questions:

- How does one relate to God?
- Can one connect directly with God? And will God respond?
- Or, must one commune through an intermediary such as the Christ, the Church or the sacraments?

These give rise to another important question:

- Does the Divine work through a human will free to follow its own direction or through a human will that has no "say" in its response or direction.

The different answers from Western and Eastern Christian Churches given to these questions determined where the Prayer developed and how it became a personal path for spiritual and religious life.

The Jewish/Christian approach insists that a chasm separates humanity from its creator; God is wholly other.

However, some Gnostics[xiv] maintain the self and the divine are identical and self-knowledge is knowledge of God. This capacity to know God through one's self is the very fiber of the Prayer of the Heart; this attitude is mystical, Gnostic and Eastern, in terms of origin, and not readily acceptable to the Western mind.

Jesus of the *Nag Hammadi Library*[xv] (a Gnostic text discovered in Egypt in 1945 whose content is traceable to the first three centuries of the Christian Era) speaks of illusion and enlightenment, not of sin and repentance as the Jesus of the New Testament does. Instead of coming to save humanity from sin, the Gnostic Jesus comes as a guide who opens the individual's access to spiritual understanding. Such awareness of illusion and enlightenment and its availability to each human being is the basis of the Prayer of the

---

[xiv] Gnosticism is a system of belief combining ideas derived from Greek philosophy, Oriental mysticism, and Christianity stressing salvation through knowledge.

[xv] *The Nag Hammadi Library*, ed. James M. Robinson (San Francisco: Harper & Row, 1977).

Heart. It denies nobody; it makes no one subservient; its internal process leads each participant to a sense of universal human equality. The one who uses the Prayer of the Heart does so hoping to become Christ-like, hoping to imitate the nature of God.

The Prayer of the Heart and the system that developed came from the Desert Fathers in the earliest monastic orders about 100 years after the death of Jesus. A group of men went into the desert of Egypt and there committed to a spiritual life based upon Christian teaching. They also avoided involvement in questioning who or what Jesus was.

They knew Jesus as a principle and that Jesus's power came from a Christological realization that lives in the heart of everyone. Their purpose was to contact that power. They wanted to discover a way to realize the same experience that Jesus had while on Earth. So they put their whole being into that endeavor. They lived solitary hermits' lives in small caves. If you have been to Jerusalem, you may have seen similar caves in the Essene area.

At that time many people lived in communities, practicing the presence of God or the living Christ as an ongoing activity. They built communities because they knew they needed to be surrounded by people with a similar consciousness if they were going to succeed in their practice. You need a supportive community to fully develop spiritually! The importance of spirituality is the practice and the commitment, not the external words, but the practice and the commitment.

These men were called "Hesychasts", which simply means "those who are in pursuit of the silence together." This was a living silence, which says "we meet together and we will carry this Prayer ongoing, in our hearts, with full devotion. And we will then watch our lives in relationship to the Prayer's work within our being."

Hesychasm is the contemplative or mystical tradition of Eastern Orthodox Christianity. The goal is to experience God directly. Hesychasm is the method of interior or spiritual prayer which leads to the mystical experience.

Hesychasm itself became the subject of serious controversy in the fourteenth century. The preceding six hundred years had been relatively clear of dissension, in terms of church squabbles, and during this time contemplation and the way of the mystic gained prominence. The teaching of Hesychasm had been first committed to paper by St. Symeon the New Theologian at the beginning of the eleventh century. St. Symeon, perhaps the noblest mystic of the Greek Church, crystallized a form of prayer which was adopted by the monks at Mt. Athos (considered to be the "seat" of interior prayer):

"Lord Jesus Christ, have mercy on me; Son of God, help me."

St. Symeon had laughed at the earnest discussions of theologians concerning the nature of God. He simply said that it was only necessary to know God.

"Possess God and you will need no books."[xvi]

"It was believed that the monastic visionary in his rapt contemplation partook of the very substance of God Himself and was surrounded by the uncreated light which was revealed on Mount Tabor at the transfiguration."[xvii]

Hesychasm was transmitted by Greek missionaries to Slavonic countries, most notably

---

[xvi] Robert Payne, *The Holy Fire* (New York: St. Vladimir's Seminary Press, 1980), p. 271.

[xvii] Williston Walker, *A History of the Christian Church* (New York: Charles Scribner's Sons, 1959), p. 213.

to Russia, where it exercised tremendous influence upon the spiritual development of the entire Orthodox world.

During three periods, the practice of the Prayer has been particularly intense: the first was during the fourteenth century; the second was in Greece during the late eighteenth century; and the third was in Russia during the nineteenth century. There also seems to be a revival in the twentieth century among the lay people in Russia.

The Prayer of the Heart draws from several powerful traditions: Gnosticism, mysticism, Eastern Orthodoxy and monasticism.

Through Gnosticism it identifies with the pursuit of knowledge (gnosis), which one gains from observation or experience. This kind of knowing cannot be taught; it can only be evoked or awakened from within. This privilege of knowing from within allowed us to pursue our own knowledge of what is, from an inner well. This removes the Church from the position of authority and bestows responsibility and opportunity on us. The Prayer of the Heart is our vehicle to pursue this inner knowledge and personal authority.

Gnosticism indicates that the ultimate object of gnosis is God; that view is also central to the Prayer of the Heart. Our experiencing God is the entire aim of the Prayer, and the process of knowing God transforms us by making us a participant in the divine existence. This belief gives us the right and declares we have the ability to relate to God directly. No mediator is needed: no church, no sacrament. With the opportunity comes dignity and freedom; God can be experienced by anyone, anywhere, at any time, on one's own merits.

The Prayer is also a vehicle for the mystical experience. References constantly call the Prayer mystical because the Prayer wraps within itself the aim for union with the Divine. Furthermore, that special sense of the Divine being everywhere, that moment where we feel embraced by Love and carried by Life, that feeling of awe at the subtlest and greatest as communicated by the mystic are the background guarantees of the Prayer—its gifts of the Spirit.

The Prayer as a mystical experience gently leads us in the direction of that God experience. The Prayer, through its image of the flame in the heart, ever flaming higher through love and attention, leads us finally to seeing only love and knowing only God in all, through all, pervading all.

As the prayer works in us and we work the prayer, our nature is altered through the subtle power of awareness. Of what do we become aware? We become aware of the corruption of our human nature caused by our accepting false images as truth. These mirages are the conditionings, veils, subterfuges of personality and relationship and beliefs, which separate us from realizing our oneness with God and our Divine Nature. In order to attain this sense of oneness with God, through awareness, we must approach selflessness whereby we no longer seek to express an existence separate from God.

Along the way, we must confront our inner darkness; and, wonderfully and mysteriously, not only let go of self, but also see our interconnection with all people as if of one body. Through our expanding consciousness we experience the light so often mentioned in religious and mystical illumination. This Divine Light is ever-present, equally in light and darkness, in all places, whether we perceive it or not.

To understand why the Prayer evolved through the Eastern Church, we need to consider how the two Christian Churches diverged in their basic concepts. Periodically there were doctrinal battles over the interpretation of the Logos (the ultimate reality) and the Christological (study of the work and person of Jesus) concept:

- Who is Jesus?
- How shall Jesus be interpreted?
- Who is Mary?
- Was Jesus truly incarnated in the flesh, or is he only Spirit?
- What is Jesus's relationship to the Father?
- How does Holy Spirit function?

The first notable distinction between East and West occurred early in the second century with different concepts of salvation. The Eastern Church believed in transformation of sinful mortality into blessed immortality. The Western Church saw salvation as the establishment of right relations with God and the forgiveness of sin.

The growing Gnostic tradition in the second century separated the two even further. Christians needed an authority on whom to declare their beliefs viable and well established in Christ. They needed a genetic code, a bloodline, which would give them distinction and strength against the syncretic and universally-absorbing Gnosticism.

Thus the church in Rome accepted the Apostolic Tradition, which purported that the Christian teachings were passed down directly from the Apostles and were preserved in the Apostolic Churches.

Further, Ireneus, the Bishop of Lyons, confirmed the line of bishops having served in Rome since Peter and Paul and established the church as the depository of Christian teaching. He declared that there could be only one church and outside that church there is no salvation. Since Rome had been the center for strengthening Christianity in this controversy, it became the prominent church, and its bishop the spokesman for all matters of the church at large.

The Eastern Church moved toward Hesychasm's basic belief that the individual could connect with God directly, without the priest or church as the intermediary. The Hesychast's contemplative way of stillness and response is the mystical tradition of Eastern Orthodox Christianity. It is the Christ-given 'initiation' into the Divine mysteries. Its focus and promise is an awakened, direct experience of God and union with Him.

And finally, the fourth powerful tradition contributing to monasticism (The Prayer of the Heart) began long before St. Symeon, the New

Theologian, committed the Prayer of the Heart to paper. Monks in the Egyptian desert adopted its practice as a way to connect with the Divine.

Monasticism in the Christian tradition had its origin in a layman's movement founded by Anthony, a native Egyptian and a Copt, born in 250. He gave away all his possessions, took up the ascetic life in his native village, and then went into solitude becoming a hermit. Anthony developed the practice of fasting, strict self-denial, and praying constantly, which was imitated by many others who either live absolutely alone as hermits or in small groups as hermits in the deserts of Nitria or Scetos.

The Cenobite[xviii] form of monasticism originated through Pachomius, born in 292. He adopted the hermit life, but, dissatisfied with its irregularities, established the first Christian monastery in Tabennisi, Egypt, ca. 315-320. In his practice all participants were knit into a single body through assigned work, regular hours of worship, similar dress, and living in cells near each other.

[xviii] A Cenobite is a member of a religious order living in a monastery or convent.

Between 360 and 379 Basil of Caesarea brought a rigid order to monastic life that became the standard for monasticism within the Greek and Russian Churches.

As a result of this combination of mystical Eastern Orthodox, Gnostic and the monastic teachings, one of the great gifts of the Prayer is its capacity to incorporate all parts of the human being without judgment. There is no separation between body and spirit. Each flows into the other, serves the other, like a dance of integration and intermingling. God is everywhere, in all parts; and through the Prayer the body and Spirit are communing and communicating that Truth each moment.

The Western tendency to honor the individual is significant and important, but we must let go of our individuality to become a part of a community, the entire human race—a humble action full of nobility and dignity. The Prayer teaches all of this understanding, the necessity of full self-identity before we can attain the state of humility. And once our personality is ready, all the Prayer asks is humility before God's Will always.

The Prayer is a vehicle of transformation. It demands that we not remove ourselves from any part of us or the world. Nothing is to be denied or rejected. It expects that we wear the Dark Night of the Soul, address our weaknesses, use our sins for learning and stepping towards love, and recognize our pain as a purging fire of renewal.

Man indeed is saved, not from the world, but with the world; and that world includes his inner world, which will be seen clearly by the Prayer carried in the Heart.

Through all of this process, through constantly carrying the Prayer in the heart, we become big enough and brave enough to be transformed through the purifying flame burning ever brighter as our attention remains in the heart. As it glows brighter, we become illumined, filled with the Light, and our human and Divine natures unite as one. But the human has not gone away or been beaten into suppression and submission. It has been fully embraced as an aspect, yes, even an expression, of the Divine evolution in each human being.

4: THE REFINER'S FIRE

"Those who are in pursuit of the silence together" were called Hesychasts. Don't think of that silence as the Unity silence! This is a living silence. The living silence says, "We meet together and we will carry this Prayer ongoing, in our hearts, with full devotion. And we will then watch our lives in relationship to the Prayer's work within our being."

Make a commitment to the Prayer! It is extremely important that you bring your mind into the heart and then carry it there fulltime, 24-hours a day. I do that. My life is based upon this belief that the practice is so powerful that my whole personality, life style, and organic environment will gradually come into alignment with the Prayer. Whatever you devote yourself to, whatever you dedicate yourself to, you become.

Now this is peculiarly unique, different from our usual spiritual life. We normally say, "I am a human being and I live in this society and this society tells me what's right and what's wrong." Then, knowing what's right and what's wrong, we decide, "Well that isn't good for me. Something else is better for me. So I will let go of this and take on something that is better for me. I will change my conditioning in the world, so that I will become a different person in here." So we look outside to determine who we should be morally, ethically, socially and as a personality. If we find ourselves cutting down our mate, we think, "Oh, it isn't very nice to cut down my mate. At Unity they teach love. So I will love my mate."

What I am about to say is psychological as well as spiritually evident. We have discovered that you can only look outside for so long in an attempt to shape your life based on the external and bring that into yourself. After a while something begins to upheave inside of you.

Haven't you noticed that? You can only be nice to your mate so long and something goes "Burp." That is the way we have usually structured our religio-spiritual life. Think about it! Think about yourself!

I remember I used to come home saying, "I want to be good. I want to be a good person." Then I would try to figure out what a good person was and it got so confusing. I didn't even know who I should be. I thought I ought to make a commitment to something.

This is different. This simply says: "You are a person living in the world. If you live your life based on that, you are in for continual ups and downs and upheavals. It really doesn't last very long and it is very frustrating. So bring your mind into your heart. Leave your mind in your heart." Over and over and over again the great spiritual teachers say that. The profound simplicity of that is so frighteningly simple most people dismiss it and leave saying, "I thought I came to learn about prayer." They didn't even hear that the beginning principle is to bring the mind into the heart.

What happens is this energy base begins to expand. It is like giving energy and attention to the sun or to a flame. As you give energy and attention to it, the flame increases. As it increases, this ball of energy gradually consumes the whole person, the whole personality, the whole ego structure, the whole environment, and integrates it with this little presence here in the heart and the spiritual teachers call it a little presence here in the heart.

This is a big theory and I'll keep repeating it. It is a huge theory. It allows you to incorporate all you have been, so that there is no separation between you and God, so that ALL becomes acceptable, so that you become free to be moved by this spiritual force.

Let me play around with you philosophically. Don't tune me out yet. What if anger is a part of God's universe? And you have been conditioned to believe that there is something wrong with anger, which causes you to judge yourself and you try to get rid of it. Yet you all profess a great statement which says, "The light of God surrounds me. The love of God enfolds me. The power of God protects me. The presence of God watches over me. Wherever I am God is." Well now, folks, I really want to get you to take a stand on your faith. Taking a stand on your faith says that you stand behind what you say. If you said, "Wherever I am God is," then there has to be some kind of movement inside of you to accept anger. The only way through anger is fully accepting it.

When you practice the Prayer of the Heart this flame becomes so big that it is willing to embrace even anger. It becomes so large that it is able to accept the presence of hatred, revenge, and even those occasional desires to kill when you are pushed.

I don't know what is going on in your head right now. What most people do when somebody dares to say this is to respond, "But if we all get angry what will happen to the world? What will happen to my dear husband or my kids, if they only knew what I really feel and how much it goes on?" Well I am going to challenge you again. Do you trust that God knows what God is doing with you? I am going to get you to stand behind your faith position and say, "I am committed to a trusting God. I trust my anger. I trust God's process in me."

Now you can do all kinds of stuff with this. "Does that mean that I blurt it out all over everybody?" Sometimes.

"Does that mean I feel bad when I do?" Sometimes.

But there is a difference. There is a little prayer in your heart that keeps you in the presence with God and allows you to accept all of yourself on this rollercoaster ride called life. And it doesn't dam you up. It gives you more of the presence of God to share.

I almost can read your minds and you're asking "and what next?"

What's next?

What's next is ... what is next.

'What's next' means you keep being led. You know that you didn't finish when you graduated from college or high school or you dropped-out. So you just keep taking a step and then another and you trust the Spirit, because, and listen, you are doing the practice.

If you are not doing the practice, you may have to fiddle around in this world, you are going to have to keep your old way of relating to the world.

Maybe you're ready to make a choice whether you want to continue your normal way of relating or try This System (based on carrying a prayer in your heart). This System leads to integration, a realization of wholeness, and tremendous spiritual freedom. Your usual system leads to control, knowing what's next, limits, and definition.

What do you want?

And it doesn't mean anything whatever you choose and I don't care, because one system isn't necessarily better or worse than the other. I do know that This System is deeper.

I began practicing the Prayer of the Heart in October 1977. I did it on a trip to Los Angeles. I didn't know what I was doing, but I knew that I had started doing this prayer and it just captured me and I knew that my life was dependent upon it. It felt like salvation. It felt like a crisis point. You've got to know that when I began the prayer rather than everything getting better it got a lot worse. If you read the great Christian mystics and saints or talk with the real students, the people who have their roots in deep spiritual traditions, they will tell you this, "If you make a commitment spiritually, you have got to make the commitment regardless of the results and without expectations." You can't walk into this if you want something better for your life. You have just got to walk into it because this is all that you have left to do. So I gave up expectations for my spiritual life.

And I would like you to know that when it got worse, I could truly relate to the man who tells the story in a marvelous book called *The Way of the Pilgrim*. I was introduced to this practice by reading about a Russian peasant with a deformed arm. He lost his wife and his life looked ruined. Not knowing what to do, he traveled by foot to Moscow where he met a Russian priest, a starn. The priest said that he knew how to help this peasant and asked him to find a place where he would have simple work to do. The priest also instructed him to say the Jesus Prayer while he was working. So the man began, "Lord, Jesus Christ, have mercy on my soul."

Now, we react to these words because we all know so much and because we've gone beyond that, which may be true or it may not be true. So the Pilgrim finds a simple little house, continues his work, while repeating the Prayer 3,000 times a day. The peasant did this and it's important for you to understand that he did it well. After he'd done it for a week he went back to the priest and said to him, "I want you to know that my world is a mess."

The reason that I say that it had begun to work is because the exact same thing happened to me. The minute I started to practice the Prayer, I realized in my total humility what a mess my consciousness was. I don't mean that in guilt. I began to see what I really thought.

What happens internally is you begin to realize where your thoughts really are running to, where the basis of your existence really is. You begin to realize how motivated you are by the lower chakras, by the sexual chakra, by the power and ambition chakra, and you begin to understand why you have jealousies and why you have needs and why you get possessive, and you begin to understand why you latch on to personalities and why they have so much power in your life, and why you are always looking for love. You begin to really see it because everything opens up within you, and you begin to be obvious to yourself.

When the peasant went back to the priest, the priest said to him, "Look, even though you can see clearly how you are and who you are, I want you to increase it—I want you to start saying it 3,600 times a day." The priest knew when you begin to penetrate the present depth of your being you've got to go through the ever-present unknown darkness of your own self. If you don't have the courage to go through it, you can never know the depths of your being. Find out what's holding you back! You've got to trust this refinement. What does it say in the book of Micah? It says, "And ye shall be purified by the refiner's fire." Well this is the refiner's fire and you make a commitment to it to practice it and to be refined.

Now that doesn't seem possible that you could say a prayer that often. Yet, the man did it. He repeated the prayer more and more times a day and gradually he discovered the wonderful trick of this little experience: if you devoted yourself to this kind of internal prayer work, your consciousness changes. When you start, you see that outside you has been this huge circle of your world—the world that you were living in that is your conditioning, your belief in illness and destruction and danger and need and ups and downs and loneliness and fear and dread and joy and love and passion and despair and disillusionment and the need for jobs and getting along with people and not getting along with people, and all those curiosities and confusions.

If you hold on to this inner Prayer of the Heart, this small inner space begins to expand. It begins to get so large, this little force that is building inside you, that IT becomes your world... and It's very simple and It's very rudimentary and It's very pure.

The uncanny occurrence is that your former world loses its power and it doesn't stay strong anymore. You become this inner space, this huge, very quiet, very peaceful internal force... just because you started doing that simple prayer in your heart and mind.

A lot of people say, "I can't do that because I have to work for a living." Well, you do this whether you are working for a living or not. You do this while making love. You do this while kissing. You do this while disciplining your kid.

You do this while writing your check. You do this while sitting and talking with a friend. You do this while driving your car. You don't just go into a little meditation room for 20 minutes a day and say, "Oh, I found God. That's it. Enough for today!" You don't just read your little *Daily Word* and say, "I did my spiritual practice for the day." There is so much more than that.

The person I was eight years ago isn't around anymore. The one I am today won't be here four years from now because the fire is burning me. It is burning me up. It isn't throwing me away. It is just continually consuming me so that I might participate in the evolutionary expanding process. Not so that I'll get better, I may be worse than I was yesterday. I hope you can understand that. But I am committed to the refiner's fire. Whenever you're refined, you have to take a good look at

— Who am I?
— How do I really function here on Earth?
— What is really going on in this mind?

You get rid of that paltry, superficial, sickening, happy self. If you stay in the happy-hearted position, where you are always keeping your world together just so you can always say, "I know God is working and the only place that God is working is where it is good," then you haven't brought yourself into the other half where you know God is working even in your darkest side. That is what happened to the Pilgrim. He entered into his dark side.

That is what happened to me. I couldn't believe it. Folks, I have done my psychological stint. I had gone through T-groups. I discovered the weakness of my personality. I have worked really hard with them. But there are deeper, darker parts of me. There are deep fears. Just being alive is fearful. There are primal parts of me like my desire to survive. There are powerful energies. There are powerful sexual energies inside me. I had to meet them. I kept saying, "You mean that is me? You mean that is what really drives me? You mean this is what I am really all about? You mean this wonderful woman who went into the ministry?" I looked into the mirror and I saw deeply through the shine, through the veneer. So the Pilgrim continues his way and so did I.

This has become so much a part of me that I cannot look out through my mind anymore but that I look out through a prayer. I can never lose myself anymore. I can't get caught in the clatter and the rumble and the rattle. You may think that is wonderful, but I want you to know it is a very difficult process that occurs. You can get very scared because you feel very alone. You don't get lost in the world anymore, but I've missed that rush. My major suggestion to you for raising consciousness is that you start practicing the presence of God, and when you do, you'll find that you will gradually have an attitude of love moving inside you. You'll always find that when you are not quite on kilter, what's wrong is that you have lost love. I know that now. Whatever the issue, wherever I'm projecting my problem any time, or however I'm feeling antsy, it has to do with losing my sense of love.

This is long term work. After entering into the Prayer of the Heart in October 1977, nearly two years later in March 1979, I was awakened with the fourth major mystical experience of my life. A luminous cross awakened me and gradually implanted itself into my breast just beneath the skin. It was awesome! Love, not human love, not good/bad love, but a power-filled love engulfed the room and laid itself inside my breast and hung there. When I awoke the next morning, I felt as if I were in love, but no longer in love with a man, but in love with a spiritual energy. I had fallen in love and my heart had been opened. It had been broken open. I knew for the first time, as it says in

Genesis, "And he shall place a firmament in the midst of the water." I have never lost it. It doesn't go away. I knew that. That is what had happened that night. A powerful force, which I had worked with such intensity to stir the embers of my soul, sowed itself within me. And it came to stay. And I knew that the firmament had been placed in the midst of my water.

5: THE ROLE OF THE MIND

In developing a prayerful attitude, it is essential that we treat the mind properly if we are to unite with our Spiritual Nature. Through our mind we can be freed from those emotional, mental, worldly issues which distract from true Oneness. Certain issues are inherent in strengthening, controlling, and sustaining one's mind:

– the activity of the mind during prayer,
– the treatment of thoughts,
– the expansion of control and discrimination, and
– the use of concentration and attention.

Understanding each of these and responding sensitively to the subtle shifts which occur as a result of prayer's inherent discipline becomes a matter of exploration and experimentation for us as seekers. People who have practiced the art of Prayer to alter their consciousness and effect a change in self-identity and the way they relate to the world emotionally and mentally are generally clear that the mind is the primary tool for this work.

The Nature of Mind

So, how should we, as students of the prayer life, see the mind?

First, teachers of the practice believe that we must honor it and not treat it simply as a research medium. Rather, working with our mind is a personal experience.

The promise is that through diligence we will come to know our mind well in terms of its function, its tendencies, and its rebellious inclinations. We will learn its content, the interconnections of thoughts and how one leads to another. We will understand causation and conditioning.

To know our mind intimately, we must study with but one goal: to master it and achieve union with God.

Little wonder that the saints and monastics struggled to control their mind and stay centered on God. We can understand more obviously that the promise of knowing God, achieving a special and blissful state of union with God, had to be worthy, possible, all-consuming and even helped by God, for the practitioner to carry on.

Attending to God

Obviously our mind's role is to attend to God. This view has been expressed by monastics, saints, and hesychasts alike. My personal experience has been that in the attending, my whole understanding of whom or what God is changes, evolves, and expands. A word, God, becomes an experience. A distant Power becomes my intimate companion and guide. An object which previously carried fear and judgment grows into a freeing, nonresistant fluid of love, bathing my every thought, action and emotion, yet never relenting in my onward movement.

Spiritual teachers are consistent in their directions: recognize the necessity for the mind always to attend to God! Banish all memory of earthly things and deeds! Constantly guard the mind against earthly concerns and stay focused! The mind then naturally "soars".

The assumption is, having released the world, our mind can return to its natural home, being with God. This of course demands that we focus inwardly, knowing this will raise our being and our general overall nature. When we withdraw our attention from the external, worldly clutter falls away. This works!

I have found that my attention alone allows outer realities to exist. If I remove my attention, the gross matter falls away, leaving my soul, my spirit, and my mind free to soar to its natural state of unification with God, Oneness, bliss, and freedom. It works - if we are ready for the arduous task and the rigors demanded.

A phenomenon of human nature hinders this desire for God. Our mind prefers to be independent. It does not want to be controlled, it has enjoyed many years of freedom, wandering where it wanted, commiserating with the emotions, responding to the ego, taking off on tangents and imaginations, delighting in the world, running from one scene to another. And now, often in time of crisis, we want to control it. The mind naturally rebels.

The Means for Attending to God

Realizing the difficulty of this task and having some appreciation for the mind's complexity, let's consider how we might bring it under our control.

– Remember that wanting to know God is the spark for this venture.

- Remember also that this spark comes from God and moves into our personal awareness and causes us to long for God.
- Also, remember that having this spark is merely the first indication of the dawn, and that our assignment is to help that dawn develop into day.

The issue then is how do we address controlling the mind.

PRACTICING THE PRESENCE

Practicing the Presence is considered by many to be the singular "tool" which, when used consistently, has the capacity to contain the mind, center its direction, and yet at the same time provide it with enough flexibility to develop a liquid freedom, often called "flow".

The first requirement for practicing the Presence is that we gather our whole mind in the heart.

Simply, this requires taking our attention and directing it to the spot immediately below our sternum. The effect is remarkable, as almost immediately we can feel energy moving to that part of our body and expanding as it moves. Now this would be an easy achievement, not very remarkable, if we had to do this only once or twice or maybe for a few moments. But teachers clearly instruct us that changes of consciousness, union with God, transformation, healing and the state of bliss and freedom do not arrive with such short "jolts." This inner work is noble, life-changing, long-term in effect. Therefore, daily consistency is imperative until our very essence adjusts to its new home in the company of God.

If our mind is to dwell in the heart for a long period, accustomed as it has been to external entertainment and chatter, it will become bored unless we give it something to do.

I suggest that you fix your mind, while established in the heart, upon the Jesus Prayer, "Lord Jesus Christ, Son of God, have mercy upon me," or lift your heart spiritually towards God. You may replace the Jesus prayer with an affirmation, mantra, image or similar tool.

An important distinction between mental thinking, supplication, or affirmative-type prayer and practicing the Presence is that practicing the Presence has an internal focus. Its content is singular, whether Jesus prayer, mantra, or affirmation, and the focus is in the heart, wherever that may be for you. It is not a series of changing and fluctuating prayer thoughts based upon the moment, the issue, the need, or the personality. It is not dualistic, seeking neither to get away from the "bad" nor reaching for the "good." Rather it is centered, focused on union with God purely by paying attention within.

Some of the saints make an occasional reference to spiritually lifting the heart towards God. Such "lifting of the heart" is not external prayer nor is it verbal prayer. Its essence rests within our mind and heart. By our willingness to dwell there, our consciousness is lifted towards God.

An analogy might be humanity's tendency to attempt to reach higher or "get to heaven" by throwing an anchor into the clouds or climbing a ladder which leans on blue sky. The anchor drops heavily; the too short ladder falls to the ground. Attention within is the key to ascension. This is like the Law of Displacement. As we gather ourselves within, bringing our mind into the heart, water (the inner prayer) is poured into our being, our vessel (consciousness) expands and rises higher and higher, filtering all that has been, cleaning it, refining it, just by filling up internally, making what has been heavy lighter. This inner prayer works like the law of displacement, naturally lifting our consciousness as we infill our being.

CONFRONTING OUR THOUGHTS

Once we begin bringing our mind into the heart and attending to an inner prayer, the work moves itself along. Immediately we begin to notice what lives within:

- thought, all of it, including its content and movement,
- thought's tendencies and connections,
- thought's tracks and sidetracks,
- thought's extensions and absorptions,
- thought's possessiveness and fantasy, and
- thought's absurdities and realities.

As we continue to watch, the desire to elevate this mass by controlling it becomes our dominant intention. The early teachers recommended banishing thought as a means for control.

Instead of banishing our thoughts (which is probably impossible anyway), I recommend noticing them, then releasing them without attaching.

When we claim our thoughts as "truth," we lose control of our mind. Our mind will wander. We simply notice the wandering, then return our attention to the Jesus Prayer. We do this as the thoughts accost our personality and mind.

Meditation is another excellent tool for observing and quieting our mind and thoughts. After much diligence, we can master this undertaking and we will have finally learned to guard our mind.

Such human-Divine interaction is so powerful that it can overcome the affects of passion and become an expression of our soul's participation in divine self-love.

ATTENTION

The discovery of our inner mystery continues deeper and deeper within. As our watching goes on, the same questions arise now in different form:

— Who is it that will recognize the thought to be released?
— What is it that will recognize the thought to be released?

With these questions comes the need for developing our attention. Attention and awareness will define what fits the nature of God and what does not.

This discovery will be an evolving, purifying, spiral process ending only when we attain union, oneness with God everywhere and always. I believe, based on my own experience, that the soul, attention and awareness are linked together on the spiritual journey.

- As our soul expands so do our attention and awareness.
- As attention and awareness expand, so does the soul.

And gradually the mental and emotional are left behind. Then, the soul blossoms and God's knowing within us flourishes, absorbing our personality, diminishing the power of conditioned reactions and behaviors, eliminating worldly reflections and profoundly altering our basic life attitudes. All of those aspects of the self dissipate in power without disappearing or leaving us stripped and empty: only God is a burning, radiant light, a developed crystallization within.

Attention is the power behind our mind. And if we find it difficult to control thought, by whatever means, catching our own attention can be like a game of hide-and-seek.

We have moved now in and out of various layers of inner life: confronting the self; thinking of God; denying thought which does not incorporate God; the inner spiritual awareness of thought and releasing that which does not fit; and attention. As the consciousness deepens, it is reflected by the very force of itself. With the deepening, earlier issues disappear and the subtleties of each layer appear to be addressed in their own timing. God's Presence indeed does the work.

A strictness and possible guilt may appear as we concentrate our attention. However, such feelings diminish with the knowledge, self-understanding, and love which grow with this process. As self-judgment naturally seems to disappear on this journey, comfort and understanding support each other, allowing attention and the prayer to do their own work on the soul, naturally. It is as if once we "dig" this far, we become aware of our natural inclination towards God, peace, and love. The process then takes over the direction and unfolds naturally.

Toward Integration

Now control, discrimination, and will have obviously been a part of mental awareness and inner prayer work. As we keep the prayer in our heart, discrimination tells us what is or is not prayerful thought and directs that which does not fit to go away. The will keeps us doing the doing.

Such clarity of what fits and what does not is easier early in the process, but once we begin carrying the prayer in the heart, our choices, discriminations, and control fade from black-and-white to an indistinct grey. This is when another system begins to operate.

The Myth of the Going-Forth recounts the Jews' flight from Egypt. It helps illustrate this other system as it begins to operate. According to this interpretation, Egypt is our body, and all who identify themselves with the body dwell in ignorance. As we come forth from the body, we then pass through the Red Sea, analogous to our animal and sensual nature. Having left the body state and crossing through the sensual nature, we still must encounter the Desert or the doubting lower mind. In the doubting mind, we can wander about, unsure of our path or direction. Through the sacrifice of Moses, the true teacher, we escape the desert and enter the Promised Land, the realm of the spiritual mind.

This myth provides a sense of the development of our more profound internal system. In the beginning stages we must use discrimination, will and control to move toward God, the "Promised Land". Selectivity, choice, guardianship, and resistance to the dominant mental and emotional patterns are parts of keeping our mind on God. Thus, we pass out of Egypt and have the strength to survive the ordeal in the desert. During this period, we choose out of fear, oftentimes based upon conditioned beliefs about what is Godly and ungodly. Our choices are based on judgment, ethics and morality. We are centered on confusion and frustration, which often result in self-judgment and flagellation. The internal is turning around, but we are using old modalities without a true sense of direction without truly knowing what is right or wrong. We need a strange kind of courage to continue without knowing the outcome or even having an assurance that this is the right practice. There is no solid ground and the further we get along the way the less ground we have to stand on.

Carrying the prayer in the heart is our means for solidity. As we carry the prayer more and more profoundly, with deeper and deeper conviction, still without knowing the outcome, we find a new ground. This is where the "natural bent" of the inner nature begins to show itself, where we first see the internal system. This ground, layer, dimension, system, or whatever we may call it, is different from anything we experienced earlier. Its content and energy come from some pool of knowledge which is universal, is totally internalized, is greater than conscience, is deeper than "gut feelings," and knows its own self without doubt. Psychology might call this realm integration. For Jung it was individuation. For humanistic psychology it was transformation. And for religion, the second birth of Spirit rather than body—the real birth that sees the light of freedom, clarity, Light itself.

This does not appear overnight. It comes quietly, in glimpses, as brief moments of freedom from the demanding nature of the earlier inner work. It occurs because the discrimination and control have become so refined that they are close to being given up and will no longer have to function. The soul now instructs us and then we will hear we are finely tuned for now.

We know that will, control, and discrimination are becoming past tense when we do not have to watch so hard, pray so constantly, work so totally. Grace, the fourth stage of prayer, is close at hand; in fact, the moments, the glimpses, are grace.

It is important to recognize the courage we require to complete the turnaround. Courage is essential because it will allow us to maintain control, activate the will, carry on the discriminatory vigilance in the state of limbo which precedes grace and freedom.

All together, this process finally leads us "beyond thought." Will, control, discrimination, judgment, conscience lose their significance, and thus, their authority. Of course, then the possibility exists of a domain beyond thought—not without thought, as often suggested—but beyond thought.

6: THE MATTER OF THE HEART

The heart is the primary recipient of our intention, mind, and attention. It serves as part of Spirit's infinite process within all human consciousness. It seems, also, as if the heart is God's secret vehicle for catapulting us into sanctity and holiness. Yet, we don't discover this secret until we have evolved enough to recognize the heart's power.

Spiritual literature indicates that mankind has entered the "age of the heart." The bell of this quality of love is so ringing everywhere that it must be an idea whose time has come. The precedent for such an investment in the heart and its gift of love appeared in pre-Christian times in the Essene communities, whose chief characteristic was the doctrine of love: love of God, love of virtue, and love of mankind.

It is important to understand that this heart is not the physical heart alone, nor to the emotional center or a personal or ethical love center. When we bring our attention into our heart, we obviously refer to our physical heart. But as we work extensively with the practice, we begin to realize that such attention is tapping also into a larger energy field, another heart.

It is clear through their writings that by connecting with their hearts the Essenes, Jesus, Valentinus, Julian of Norwich, St. Teresa of Avila, St. John of the Cross, St. Catherine of Genoa, and others underwent a mighty, healing, totally unifying and interconnecting experience, a process larger than the personal, possibly the next evolutionary stage of the human species. I understand this "larger" heart to be the vehicle of the new age so often refers to: the instrument for developing the new ground and dimension.

For thousands of years before the time of Jesus, Eastern mystics discovered the body has seven centers of power (chakras), and the heart is the fourth. Ram Dass explains this heart chakra as "the first one into the transcendent state."[xix] It seems to me this involves a true cross-over in our evolution, a leap from solar plexus (third chakra) to heart (fourth chakra) which parallels the Ophic myth about Exodus and crossing the Red Sea.

[xix] Ram Dass, *The Only Dance There Is* (New York: Anchor Press. 1974), p. 82.

Once we move our focus to the heart, there are no guarantees, except a sense of the power in the heart, whether physical and spiritual or literal and ethereal. My personal experience is that carrying the prayer in the heart clearly opens our physical and spiritual center, bringing powerful resources of energy for impersonal loving and all its facets, healing, and being. The practice has led to numerous mystical experiences and a general expansion of my state of consciousness and being. It has been, truly, the most special event in my life.

Nature of This Love in the Heart

Writers who talk about Love, the Heart, the Flame (all the same essence) generally agree that this is not a one-way process. As much as you want God, God wants you. As much as God is in each of us, each of us is in God.

We may seek God arduously, yet never feel this mutual seeking from "above"; thus the need for courage and the resolve to continue whether we feel God's Presence or not, trusting that we will find His grace, whenever it is His will. We and God meet by Divine appointment, an appointment often referred to as grace.

God creates all life as objects of Divine love. As humans, we are aware that our true purpose is union with God. It is clear that our inherent nature is to know God through love for Him and His love for us—the way of the heart.

Our love expresses itself as eros (a desire to possess God) and agape (the deliberate desire to give ourselves to God).

Man and all living things exist through the power of God. In other words, our life is God; although we may not yet be conscious of that fact, life is empowered by God. We experience fear and anxieties when we are not consciously aware of God's empowerment. Our lack of awareness leads us to self-dependency, aloneness and smallness, whereas spiritual love leads us to know our interconnection with and in God. Such love is not of the passions, but is of another level, the heart.

A Process for Becoming Aware of What Is

This flame in the heart is always present in all creatures; however, only in human form is it capable of becoming conscious. Yet, apparently, it does not come into our awareness until the conditions are "right". This is our Divine appointment.

It is impossible to explain the necessary conditions, for they are entirely individual. Still there are similarities, insofar as they often occur when we are in crisis, in the midst of boredom or supreme success, or upon completion of physical/social/emotional/mental development. The flame appears sometimes when none of these conditions are present, as if by accident. Obviously only God knows. However, when it appears, we recognize it and our life's focus shifts. The flame must be followed, with all of our will and desire, beyond sense or sensibility.

Theophan the Recluse provides cautious guidance:

Feeling towards God—even without words—is a prayer... Guard this gift of feeling, given to you by the mercy of God. How? First and foremost by humility, ascribing everything to grace and nothing to yourself... Secondly, dwell in grace and do not turn your heart or thought to anything else except from necessity. Be all the time with the Lord. If the inner flame begins to die down a little, immediately hasten to restore its strength.[xx]

[xx] *The Art of Prayer*, ed. Igumen Chariton of Valamo, trans. E. Kadloubovsky & E.M. Palmer (London: Faber & Faber, 1966), p. 60.

Once again we return to practicing the Presence, or the Jesus prayer: carrying the prayer in the heart. We develop the flame by entering this place and staying there until we understand this is all there is to do or will ever be to do.

The prayer is the process of transformation and evolution; and transformation/evolution is the process of Prayer. The simplicity of this practice is difficult for us to comprehend; yet, if we only keep our attention in the "heart," all growth and results will come.

There are few attempts to explain what is going on mechanically, psychologically, or even soulfully; or why this "doing" works as it does. Enticingly the monastics, saints, and Hesychasts only beckon, luring us, encouraging us through the example of their life and presence, assuring us in the doing. The power of such an activity might be called the affirmation of one's essential being.

In so doing we gain the capacity for joy; not the joy of fulfilled desire, but of a soul lifted above every circumstance. Whether we call this "affirming our essential being" or "carrying the prayer in the heart," both attest to an activity we carry on imperviously, without regard for circumstances, conditions, personalities, past, or future. We focus only on the present and attend to the flame.

The power of that flame, when fully developed, enlightens all issues and blesses us as we carry it. Such an act demands much of us, including the letting go of expectation and trusting only our inner life force. The Hesychasts and Gnostics, the Essenes and Pharisees, the Stoics and Spinozans, the saints and mystics, knew that their demand is both absurd and correct.

Desire

Continuing this practice requires our intense desire, which we must refine, polish, and evolve. It must be equal to loving only God. We are clearly aware that desire is the impetus of our life's activity and manifestations. Desire can take us to any place in mind, and when well-developed can bring us just about anything we want. Yet, desire can become a trap as its tendencies draw our attention away from the heart and the universal desire, God. The tendencies draw us in the direction of acquisitions, sensual fulfillment, greater and more dramatic highs, and new and more romantic love objects. As we fulfill one desire, we seek another, greater, sensual pleasure and satisfaction.

Understanding the nature of desire and becoming committed to directing it towards God alone, we are prepared to move inward, to the heart. It seems that such awareness and commitment would make the journey easier; yet, once again, our physical nature has a will of its own.

Our desire not only must be turned from external to internal, but it also must be coaxed, supported, trained, nurtured, taught to move forward into the unknown. Aspiration towards God and courage must join hands within us to accomplish this portion of our journey: first it was the mind, then the attention, now desire.

Out of such investment comes a truly remarkable state: the open heart, the heart "that loves God for no motive except to love God." It is the loving state beyond conditions or proof, without the dualist's demands for the good, without deadline or definition. There are no conditions upon which love of self, love of others, love of the conditions themselves is based. This is unconditional love, the transcendent state.

We have given up all without giving up the dance of life itself; and yet we have given up nothing as we hold totally to God without requirement or even understanding all that involves.

We come to know what it is to desire all, attain and achieve it, resign it and then continue on in infinite connection with God alone. Before concluding these dramatic effects of building the flame in the heart, let's pause and consider one of the most difficult areas of human experience, the emotions, and their evolution in our practice.

Passionlessness

But first, let's discuss "passionlessness". This is a state assumed essential by most who have shared the journey of the heart.

When taught from a position of authority, passionlessness has often been misunderstood, leaving many seekers feeling guilty and fearful. When I first encountered the idea twelve years ago, I felt a chill of fear ripple through my nervous system.

The key to experiencing the larger values of life is to conquer our emotions. Then we can experience spiritual truths and realities and know our true feelings. Few people can appreciate the sense of such an implication and lacking this appreciation, understandably, most turn their backs on even the hope of achieving passionlessness. Yet it is in the passionless state that we can best reach unification, Oneness. Only after achieving passionlessness can we attain essential wisdom, true contemplation, and the knowledge of the One and Indivisible.

This may seem absurd to us; but even that reaction is an obvious deception, our mind playing tricks to keep us from unification and essential wisdom.

> *"A man who has not become free from passions, does not even know what passionlessness is, and does not believe there can be anyone like this on earth. For if a man has not first renounced himself and has not exhausted his (being) for the sake of this...life, how can he imagine that anyone else has done this, to acquire passionlessness?"*[xxi]

Passionlessness is a safe haven for a heart free from thoughts. Herein one experiences grace, which passion may have caused us to forsake. The quality of passionlessness is pure love; here we participate in the infinite spiritual love with which God contemplates and loves Himself. We become active in the Spirit by entering through the door of the flame in the heart.

[xxi] Writings from the *Philokalia* on Prayer of the Heart, trans. E. Kadloubovsky and E.H. Palmer, 2nd ed. (London: Faber and Faber, 1954), p. 109.

Human Emotional Content

The teachers of the Prayer of the Heart clearly define human emotional content, but devote little time to what produces it. They focus, instead, on what must be put aside.

In *The Dark Night of the Soul,* St. John of the Cross deems such imperfections as gluttony, anger, lust, etc., as the movement of God and said it is an honor to become more aware of these subtleties of the inner life. He then prods us to take on such imperfections as pride, avarice in the spiritual sense, luxury, wrath, spiritual gluttony, spiritual envy and sloth, as a means to becoming ready for God's love.[xxii]

In looking at these "wickednesses" and natural passions, it is important for us to consider the true intention of such demands:

– to bring our mind and heart to God;
– to experience Divine union of the soul with God;

[xxii] Saint John of the Cross, *The Dark Night of the Soul*, trans. E. Allison Peers, 3rd ed. (New York: Image Books, 1959), pp. 39-60.

– to develop the pure flame of love in our heart beyond passions.

To achieve such refinement requires our serious commitment. Not everyone wants such a state and few have an inkling of the possibility of unification with God, even though it is inherent and waiting, resting in each of us.

If, however, we agree to participate, then we are like the athlete who realizes eight hours a day practice is no small sacrifice for a chance at the Olympics. Like the athlete, we must understand why we are practicing. If we do not understand why we practice then we perform the very same exercises in a state of resistance and doubt. Performing the exercise with resistance or in doubt can create actual damage to our emotions and psyche and require many years of healing and resting before our soul can resume its journey, if ever. However, if we can accept the sacrifice of dedicated practice, then we can at least respond to such total perceptions and expectations.

Purification

Human emotions serve a purpose in everyone. They serve a purpose and yet, at the same time, as we evolve in spiritual awareness and intent being passionless is prescribed as the next step. How, then, can we attain this state?

Some attempts are like taking a mild anesthesia for the emotions, slaying our hideous demons, repeating denials and self-flagellation. These attempts lead to strangling life rather than developing a glowing flame in the spiritual heart. Such systems have quashed action and creativity or have finally erupted in outraged, deprived Christians. These methods, created out of ignorance, disregard the emotional life as a pathway to the flame in the heart.

Our motivation to become passionless must move from within, not be imposed upon from without, as an antidote for our sins or those of society. Thus it comes through our awakening soul; and it moves into our mind and the heart as a result of our praying much as well as counseling our mind to be quieter and directing our attention again and again inwardly. We direct our attention inward by thinking of God and overcoming our personal weaknesses, and gently assisting desire's tendencies toward God alone. Only such a yearning, such a simple thought can come through those of us who are now willing to be purified. We must be ready to be egoless without being scared to death. We must be able to stand the subtle learnings, which we must gather to be humbled before God.

And how shall we be purified as our awakening soul calls now, "It's time to move again, deeper, clearer, closer, and purer"?

The answer is "Accept."

Accept what?

Accept who we are now.

There is a demand for Oneness and unification, and on the way we recognize that God loves us, wants us, and is the shaper of this journey—ever more aligning us with His will. We must give ourselves to God and in doing so we are purified. In the giving we accept ourselves and see all we are as totally in God.

This process of purification, blended with a keen understanding of its intention, allows the heart to burn ever brighter, since that which could limit its light is accepted through awareness and so is rendered meaningless. It is rendered meaningless because nothing has been destroyed. Instead everything has been incorporated as a part of God's love, as a part of the whole.

THE ART OF PURIFICATION

The art of purification is one of the least understood disciplines despite a number of writers having addressed the topic. St. John of the Cross, in *Dark Night of the Soul,* refers to two kinds of purgation, both difficult and painful:

> *The one night of purgation will be sensual, wherein the soul is purged according to sense, which is subdued to the spirit; and the other is a night or purgation which is spiritual, wherein the soul is purged and stripped according to the spirit, and subdued and made ready for the union of love with God. The night of sense is common and comes to many: these are the beginners; and the night of the spirit is the portion of very few, and these are they that are already practiced and proficient.*[xxiii]

The pain of purgation is real and many of us try to avoid it. But if we have the courage to confront this challenge, we do benefit from purification. We may receive at least four powerful gifts from

---

[xxiii] Saint John of the Cross, *The Dark Night of the Soul*, trans. E. Allison Peers, 3rd ed. (New York: Image Books, 1959), p. 61.

such effort: fulfillment, a grasp of the eternal, illumination, and "burning in the Spirit".

I. Fulfillment

Earlier I suggested that aspiration towards unification with God is a major driving force within all life. A part of that drive and its increasing awareness is our sense that there are poignant moments in life where, if we respond to the potential in that moment, our life becomes different and everything changes. Purification, including its pain to the ego, provides such a moment spiritually and leads to fulfillment of our life.

II. A Grasp of the Eternal

Woven into every great religion and philosophy is the teaching that if we can give up everything, then we gain everything.

> *He who finds his life will lose it, and he who loses his life for my sake will find it.*[xxiv]

Many have been willing to accept such a demand in the hope that everything means goods or

---

[xxiv] Matthew 10:39, Revised Standard Edition of the Bible.

relationships or victories or health. But this level of purification—resignation, total yielding of the personality to the moment as an open acceptance of Divine Will whether good or bad, without expectation — surpasses the material, seeable end. Purification cleans out each of us who dares to take it on:

- it frees us from all expectations;
- it pulls our ego up short to its own assumptions, comparisons, self-estimations, and separatist activities;
- it awakens our minds and emotions to their tedious definitions and survival techniques.

All of this is the gift of the purifying process. It makes the eternal sense in all things and at each moment available to be grasped by mind, heart, ego, and personality.

III. Illumination

The final gifts of purification will remind the reader again of the flame in the heart. The pure heart opens the way to illumination. St. John of the Cross clearly explains:

> *This dark night of loving fire, as it purges in the darkness, so also in the darkness (it) enkindles*

the soul...For cleanness of heart is nothing less than love and grace of God.... (W)hen it illumines man,... it illumines him,... according to his nature. It plunges him into darkness and causes him affliction and distress, as does the sun to the eye that is weak; it enkindles him with passionate yet afflictive love, until he be spiritualized and refined by this same fire of love; and it purifies him until he can receive the union of this loving infusion.[xxv]

IV. Burning in the Spirit

Burning in the Spirit is unification, grace, Divine union of the soul with God. This is not necessarily a culmination. It is one of the gifts available. It does not arrive and remain; more than likely, it comes and it goes.

BECOMING PURE

A pure heart is one that burns in God without any

[xxv] Saint John of the Cross, *The Dark Night of the Soul*, trans. E. Allison Peers, 3rd ed. (New York: Image Books, 1959), pp. 136, 138-139.

sense of separation, regardless of internal or external conditions.

Acceptance is a key to purification, and God's hand is working (loving us) even while we work toward (loving) God. It is essential that we act from a state of loving God, or of practicing the Presence. Our attention must not be placed anywhere else. If we will only love God, the activity of loving God tells us what to see, refine, and do. No intellectual effort is involved; Spirit is the activator.

Thus we become ready for the disciplines of straight and narrow, pruning, discrimination, and trust.

- The straight and narrow is that difficult recognition that some parts of our personality/self must go; we cannot have everything, be everything.
- Expansion comes through refining, limiting, and becoming single-pointed. The work of purification is a pruning that we participate in as a loving, gentle activity. We must not act harshly. Our awakened Spirit, not by our conditioned mind or emotions, brings to our attention the next bit of foliage to be pruned.

- Discrimination is needed in this work. The limbs of the mental-emotional-behavioral domain are not to be lopped off, but rather are to be tended gently and lovingly until it is their good fortune (and God's too) to grow and expand in an even larger expression. As they expand, rather than disappear, they merge into the whole environment.
- We must trust that purification is its own being and knows what is doing of itself.

DETACHMENT

Step by step, detachment occurs as a part of our process, a natural result of our practicing the Prayer of the Heart. We also have an equal, compensating desire to hold on. In this push-pull action, our soul relentlessly surges towards union.

Old symbols and standards must go. Conglomerations of thoughts, and their triggering beliefs, must go as well. So must the masses of emotional energy around which we build our self-image go. Every internal form which might indicate ego demands, every belief which separates the personality from total commitment and submission to God, must go as well. Again, we naturally resist this releasing and letting go.

Even the Christ must leave—always the lesser is replaced by the higher—if our personality can allow itself to detach and trust. The comforter which comes is not necessarily the sense of comfort which our present day meaning attaches to it, but rather it means a rousing force which kindles the flame in our soul. What the personality once believed was the highest attainable must now be seen as an opportunity for detachment.

This experience is like to a chrysalis hanging, caught quietly between one completed state and another, still uncertain. It is essential that we accept the intermediate state of detachment as necessary, for through it comes our pure heart, our sense of freedom, our giving to life its own self so it can be what it is, and thereby be ever experienced as Godly.

Our call, then, is to detach, fully, moment by moment. The last second is gone; the next is unknown; and the place between feels like a nebulous nothing of waiting. Yet this place of the open soul, the pure heart, is also the place of non-separation between me and Thee, and into that space come guidance, intuition, wisdom, and seeing beyond common reality to Reality.

Faith

Purification leads to the open heart. And who is the person with the open heart? How does this one live, what is the matrix of his being? The matrix is absolute faith. It is the faith that lives in the midst of fear and hope; it is a faith beyond duality, maybe even beyond God.

It is important to note that this faith is not enacted by the courageous, death-defying hero; rather, it is a quiet, simple activity of love. It is a triumphant faith: not a faith which has changed the contents to emblazon the landscapes, but a faith which glows without the personality.

Such faith has transcended right and wrong in bits and pieces. It has accepted the possibility of no God and recognized the possibility of more than God. It has encompassed all aspects of life and personality without grimace, or judgment, or manipulation, or explanation to fit our personal rules of the game. Its rules have become universal according to Divine Will. It lives fully in the moment without ridicule of the past or expectation of the future.

This is a rare and special faith, attained by full risk-taking, based upon a complete sense of the dignity of our life. It is capable of being measured slowly and mastered perfectly, through the Prayer of the Heart.

Prayer of the Heart

7: TRANSFORMATION

The intensity of carrying the prayer within the heart has its affects. These touch every phase of our life, including our attitude (essentialness), behavior, relationships to people, and basic responses to good/evil, sex/pleasure, and life/death. We experience both suffering and glory.

Undertaking this journey with the intent on altering our personality, adding to our intellectual abilities, attaining healing, or straightening out our life, may backfire and create anguish. Our only purpose must be to love God.

With our only intent being to love God, our heart will gradually open and purify, then nothing can separate us from the Presence of God. Not because nothing is trying, but because we cannot be apart from God under any circumstances.

Essentialness

We each have a philosophical window through which we view the world, our essential nature, composed of beliefs and conditionings. We build

115

our life and set its direction based on our essential orientation. Rarely do we question our perspective or shift to a more expanded view.

The practice of 'the prayer' opens us to inquiring and growth, which often causes much of our fear and suffering. Through the prayer we move to new, larger perspective or "essentialness" made up of

- nonduality,
- obedience,
- humility, and
- attention in the heart.

NONDUALITY

When we first set foot on the path we are attached to our self and we presume to know what is good or bad. As we practice 'the prayer' we begin moving into a new, larger perspective. It is a remarkable feat to concentrate our whole intention while releasing any assumption that we know what is good or bad for ourselves, our life, or others.

Carrying the prayer in our heart leads us to nonduality, this state of openness, and the gifts of illumination, light, and bliss. Such a state of mind and being, such essentialness, indicates that we have traveled far on our journey and have built a firm foundation.

To understand and accept such teaching, we must develop a mature soul. After indulging in ego delight and experiencing its follies and inconsistencies, we are willing to forsake the demands for a good "show" or a good result. We accept the whole process, trusting in Spirit's broader design for unfoldment.

This does not deny our feeling of pain, but suggests that we can let go of suffering. These uncomfortable situations may occur through no fault of our own, but they can push us to experience ourselves. This is a key to the depth we can discover in solitude and silence.

OBEDIENCE

One of the joys of leaving childhood is we no longer need to submit to someone else's authority. Hopefully, we gain our own authority and self-identity—become our own master. It is a strange paradox that once we gain some semblance of self-authority, our spiritual path leads us through the Prayer of the Heart to becoming obedient again. But this time we

117

surrender to a Higher Authority, doing what we have been given to do without fear or demand.

This Higher Authority:

- gives and takes away,
- designs the circumstances and the process,
- designates who will provide the experiences and in what order, and
- establishes both the blocks and the passageways.

In obedience, we develop essentialness which has moved beyond question, beyond self-will or self-plan, and even beyond defining God's Presence. For God's Presence is All and in all, and we must walk with an obedient heart. This process is, simply, carrying the Cross.

HUMILITY

God is seeking us as much as we are seeking God. If we forget this, then our pride arises and deprives us of the gust of God's wind to carry us aloft.

Humility means, in a spiritual sense, withdrawing our will and accepting what is happening in this instant as Divine. We trust God's help and guidance, moving ahead with courage and confidence. Such believing is not future or past; it is trusting that whatever is, is part of God's plan.

Worldly judgment must not enter. Humility as an inner point of essentialness requires infinite balance. Humbly, we go forward confident in God's Presence and assistance. We are not cowardly in our actions, neither giving up nor accepting the worst. Instead, we let go of self's conditioned requirements step-by-step and accept what is, preferring neither the best nor the worst. We move ever forward, believing.

ATTENTION IN THE HEART

Our essentialness carries the prayer in our heart full-time. Although few teachers refer to the effects of such activity upon the personality, there are warnings this is neither for personal gain nor external change.

Personally, I have become quieter. Such quietness affects my poise. My need for worldly acceptance and recognition diminishes. A softness and hue of adaptability gather and become a visible part of my demeanor.

My attention in my heart becomes obvious in my eyes, my movements and gestures, and in my choice of words, eating habits and treatment of other life forms. A sense of universal kindness pervades my being and emotionalism gradually dissipates. Now there is room for God.

Behavior

The work of the prayer does create behavioral changes, even though this is not our goal.

Of course one such change is our unification with God. Although this connection is our underlying motive for the work, it is not accomplished quickly; and, once attained, it is not continually apparent.

Here is another paradox. We go forward without expectation yet we know we will receive help in going forward and that assistance is the activity of God.

We do not strive for the "good" any longer, nor do we start with the intention of becoming good or mystical. If we act from such intention, we cause pressure that builds pride by not acknowledging God's help. Yet, underneath it all, God continues to nudge our soul along and that nudge is felt as a hungering to dwell in God's Presence. God in turn desires us to be present with Him. It is a dance which humanity agrees to dance with God when its time is come. It is a dance undertaken without promise or hope; yet, each of us knows that the dance will end in unification. [xxvi]

To provide the necessary support to live a gentle, prayerful, attentive, aware, sensitive life, monastics founded several communities which were built upon spiritual values. Each community had its rituals, spiritual values, and disciplines. Many groups were not identified with a specific religion and yet were devoted to spiritual values and principles in their daily lives, while fortifying themselves through community shared living.

These communities designed practices to support a life devoted to prayer while continuing to live in the world. For example, the Desert Fathers demonstrated this lifestyle, which enabled the individual to enrich his spiritual life by living among others with similar attitudes and intentions. This monastic order was devoted to hesychia (quiet) attained through total prayer. We might find their guidelines helpful in our own dedicated prayer practice.

[xxvi] Carol Ruth had a lovely Boston accent. She always described this dance as a "dhance with the Divine." Even now, my dhance with the Divine has a Boston lilt to it.

1. Letting go of our possessions, whether as an internal activity involving our mind and emotions or as an external action relating to objects;

2. Gathering with others of like mind who are willing and committed to disciplines and rituals which nourish spiritual attitudes and habits;

3. Satisfying our need for food and work under a common roof to lighten the essential responsibilities for living;

4. Establishing specific hours for praying together and setting aside other, more flexible hours, for private study;

5. Keeping our home, clothing, and environment simple and free from distractions;

6. Devoting one day of the week to pay special attention to God through meeting, fasting, and praying together;

7. Expressing love, peace and kindness to all forms of life;

8. Practicing continence, inner cleanliness,
   purity, and meekness before God;

In addition to these behavioral guidelines, the
monks were to: do the doing, carry the prayer
always, and constantly seek unification with the
Divine.

We might assume that if we pay attention to God
with our mouth, mind, heart, and actions and
follow the monks' lifestyle, God will smile down
in His benevolence and give us a free ride. Yet,
the work must be done alone, consistently,
sincerely, and always. Only those who seek grace
and work to attain it will experience it.

It is even possible for us to drop by the wayside,
to lose what we have gained, and to have to begin
again even though we truly can never lose grace.

Relationships To People

Carrying our attention in our heart, ever
developing love toward God, does not lead to
lack of caring for our fellow men. Rather, our
intention is to become more loving of others
through loving God. This frees us from the
judgment which separates us from each other.
We must integrate love of all beings with love of
self or our unresolved, non-integrated bits and

pieces of personality will sabotage our hope for unification.

Many people—whether through mystical side-paths, monastic orders, or religious freneticism and fanaticism—have used spiritual ideals to avoid encountering self and integrating both their positive and negative sides.

They opt for kindness and positiveness, affirmations of good, and denials of bad in themselves and in all creatures. This looks fine at the distance, but when contacted up close, there is a weak philosophy and defensive texture. There is fear and resistance. Only beauty fits their structure. The depth of meeting their dark side, which can lead to fullness and completion, is clearly missing. Such people are half (only the good), not whole (integration of good and evil). Their love is based upon their terms, defined by how they define "good". Only a part of them is available to love or be loved. They withhold the remainder behind a veil of fright, unexplored, undeveloped, unwholified. This is a selfish love because a portion is hidden, separated, not available, kept for self and away from others.

Jesus of Nazareth taught as the second commandment, "Love your neighbor as yourself."[xxvii] If there is some portion of ourselves which we do not accept, then we cannot love that portion in another. By integrating all parts and potential for wholeness into a self-identity through understanding, our personality becomes ready to let go of its very identity. A higher Self can now replace the smaller self.

As we begin to let go of our personality's identity, we enter a state of readiness. This state of readiness, this sense of a new way of relating to humanity, comes gradually. We now desire to exhibit the subtleties of kindness and tenderness toward all life, at all times, by letting go of belief upon belief, habit upon habit, conditioning upon conditioning. We move from love and beyond conscience or social manipulation. Our being is transforming our personality and our behavior.

This kindness is not coercive or manipulative, even in the name of God. We become increasingly more humble, for only God's will is active in events, timing and personality. We are

---

[xxvii] Matthew 22:39, Revised Standard Edition of the Bible.

quieter for what is there to say when there is no personal self to project or defend?

As this phenomenon occurs, a presence/ Presence appears which stands within the personality (not in place of), and those who experience it/It feel love/Love.

A final behavior is non-special love. In a precious moment, Julian of Norwich asked for guidance in caring for an individual, but at first received nothing. Then, the answer came, as if from a friendly mediator, to behold God in all things rather than in any particular thing. From this she realized that holding no one as "special" is our highest presently-known relationship with others. This concept has been present for thousands of years in a society which cannot—will not—and does not yet have the ability to manifest it.

Basic Life Responses

Ultimately every area of life is affected by practice of the prayer. Spiritual literature hardly mentions the prayer's influence on sexuality, pleasure, or death. The monastic orders' discipline and life style made reference to such behaviors and attitudes unnecessary. Some writers imply or clearly state that sexual interest declines. Others encourage us to become celibate because pleasure can be absorbing and self-defeating. Others also encourage us to understand that death is an equal part of life—a state we should embrace in which we continue purifying and expanding.

Sin and evil, on the other hand, have received extensive attention from spiritual writers. In many teachings sin is a dark demon sent by the devil. Knights of valor are needed to vanquish sin and keep the human soul safe. Such protectors are usually the ministers, priests, witch doctors, and shamans who assist in our great travail. By carrying the prayer in the heart, we come to understand sin is an essential part of the whole.

In fact, if we run from sin, avoid its gift to our personality, and see life negatively as a result, then we are displaying cowardice. Thus, sin is a vehicle for growing and learning. It is an action of the universe, of God, not to be feared or run from, but rather to be encountered. We can engage sin and use it to grow, because life itself incorporates its own capacity to overcome.

Sin and evil are a part of the whole, not separate from God's rightfulness. We experience both when we refuse to give ourselves completely to God and to accept the Oneness that God has already given us. Thus, it is through judgment and conditionings that we obstruct what is. God's love, grace, is everywhere; but, through self-will, ego demands, and desires, we create a barrier that causes us to feel deficiency and pain.

However, at the same time, sin comes full circle. Even in our not beholding God's love and suffering the consequent pain, we are purged and see more clearly what we have missed by believing in "sin." Sin is a part of God's process which brings our soul closer still—to see that there is no sin.

Pain

While impacting our essentialness, behavior, and basic life responses, the practice of the prayer clearly carries with it some painful experiences. Our journey does include the richness and feeling of well-being which come with purification and detachment. It even includes an element of pride and a feeling of accomplishment which provide energy and motivation for keeping the attention in the heart. But there are also specific painful affects which attend carrying the prayer in the heart. The two most often encountered are fatigue and aridity.

FATIGUE

People engaged in this method of prayer know well the element of fatigue, but that does not stop them. Fatigue is common to all, and unless we understand and accept that, it can quickly turn us away in frustration, anger and fear.

I, too, became weary. Yet this forced me to read and practice until I fully accepted what was given. Anyone practicing the prayer in the heart must make a commitment to "leave" the world and seek constant contact with Spirit as It relates to and identifies with the world through us. This places a tremendous stress upon our system and causes us both physical and emotional fatigue. All we can do is wait patiently for our energy to return so we can grasp the next rung of the ladder, placed there by the loving hand of Spirit.

As we learn to trust, as we develop absolute faith, as we die to self and personal will, we learn to quietly wait. Our work ethic (so well taught in the Western world) dies. Our sense of control and choice is lost; bare naked. We prepare to live by the Spirit, in the heart.

Our fatigue is caused by:

— loss,

- feeling alone and different, and
- being plunged into a new consciousness where we see one thing and lose sight of another so that we can no longer describe anything.

St. John suggests, "If those souls to whom this comes to pass knew how to be quiet at this time, and troubled not about performing any kind of action, whether inward or outward, neither had any anxiety about doing anything, then they would delicately experience this inward refreshment in that ease and freedom from care."[xxviii]

All the teachers and saints have only one answer: bring the attention down into the heart and there speak the prayer again; then life will move on and strengthen you. The practice works; life becomes less threatening, and solidarity builds within.

ARIDITY

Fatigue and aridity lie close together. As fatigue

[xxviii] Saint John of the Cross, *The Dark Night of the Soul*, trans. E. Allison Peers, 3rd ed. (New York: Image Books, 1959), p. 66.

sets in and we can seemingly go no further, the gray desert of aridity appears. Those who know expect aridity to come with fatigue. It can be so severe that it affects the health. It can be so intense that it causes us to believe, "I perish."

Narrowing, which is obvious in fatigue, intensifies into aridity. Fatigue takes away our capacity to fight, resist, turn back, or hope for better. Our mind, emotions and body become dry and incapacitated. Yet, as our soul gains patience and understanding, we see this total action as loving, essential, like being narrowed down, hollowed out, stripped bare, or pressed into finer wine. We gain the strength to know completely, the only way to Oneness and unification with the Divine is through the transformation of our body, mind, and emotions. Thus, we are ready for the deeper constraints of aridity.

I. Functions of Aridity.

Aridity is an obvious part of our soul's natural growth. It is the result of conventional forms and meanings. Aridity is the result of actions and words and of reliable beliefs and other methods of the world. It is even the result of religions losing their meaning and value.

Not understanding this, nearly all religions and philosophies do not prepare us for the arid void. They are hoping somehow to avoid the pain of stretching into nothingness for the sake of expansion into the unknown. Religions promise joy and enthusiasm and goodness and mercy. Their failure to acknowledge aridity causes us to resist when we encounter this portion of our journey.

When we do not lovingly accept aridity, agony follows. Our desire to keep our spiritual journey light and easy denies the dark and heavy portion of the universe and deprives us of personal and spiritual depth.

Aridity annuls our sense of self. Aridity assists us in discovering our inner capacity for survival with God alone. The creative journey leads from fatigue to aridity and into a dark night of solitude, where we discover and experience the gifts of the Spirit. This season of aridity strengthens our core and makes us strong through the heat of pain; but we are still malleable in God's hand.

This strengthening deepens as humility expands again. As we require less and less, our humble heart awakens; and, contrary to usual thinking, more of life is available to us. This strengthening forms us into someone who can be in the midst of squalor and absurdity or regality and holiness, who can design a Sistine Chapel or lay a simple mason's block. It forms a person who can eat with publican and sinner or a pope of Rome, and not count the difference, but treats each equally.

II. The Second Dark Night of the Soul

Finally, aridity creates the environment in which a second dark night of the soul may occur. Earlier I referred to the dark night of the senses in relation to purification. This dark night, as a function of aridity, is the dark night of the spirit.

St. John recounts having left the first dark night we feel a sense of relief and freedom and readily find in our "spirit the most serene and loving contemplation and spiritual sweetness without the labour of meditation."[xxix]

Although this stage may last for years, the purgation of our soul is still not complete. New aridity, darkness and peril (sometimes more intense than those of the past) arise and

---

[xxix] Saint John of the Cross, *The Dark Night of the Soul*, trans. E. Allison Peers, 3rd ed. (New York: Image Books, 1959), pp. 91.

foreshadow our dark night of the spirit. The first dark night accommodated sense to spirit, but did not unite spirit with God. The Spirit still wants more of our soul, but our soul is not yet strong enough to undergo Divine union.

The sensual part is still too prominent in our awareness and desire. "Root" habits and affections which the first dark night was unable to penetrate remain. There is a natural roughness which we acquire from having been involved in the world. We are distracted and clinging to the world. There is an imprint on our being from having experienced the usual worldly life. The second dark night will polish away these habits and senses, leaving a fresh, willing, and nearly self-knowing soul available for the Presence. Our soul, however, is not aware of this as it prepares for its final cleansing.

Solitude

Solitude goes hand in hand with fatigue, aridity, and the dark night. In solitude we strengthen our inner being. In solitude our last grasp on self dies. Solitude is clearly a gift granted to a few through intense prayer work and devotion.

CONTENT & ENVIRONMENT OF SOLITUDE

It is easy to find pockets of rest in our journey and remain there self-satisfied, glowing in wafts of pleasure and sensations of God's gifts. St. John especially warns of this trap. The receptive space following the dark night of the sense is one such pocket. As rejoicing and fulfilling as this state is, we are not complete. We are riding the crest of the wave. There is more hidden deeper within.

St. John counsels us to not remain stuck here, but to allow the nurturing work of fatigue, aridity, the dark night and solitude to lead us to the "perfect" state. The pain and tedium may require us to invest hours, weeks, months or possibly years to meet the demand for the increased humility needed to proceed to union with God.

We enter into this inner chamber of the heart through an empty and frightening narrow hole. Even greater than the anxiety in the empty void, in solitude we face the fear of dying to our self.

This is the beauty and integrity of solitude, if we are willing to accept our whole inner being. This narrow passage culminates in the death of our self to all that we have acquired and feel we need to protect. This self, in the place of solitude, dies to its own self-knowledge so the Presence, the Christ, the inner Light of Illumination may live through it. And it dies a painful death. We must unwrap every layer of conditioning, every memory, every web of conviction from around our soul.

ACTION IN SOLITUDE

In solitude we are quiet, watching, but internally active. Spiritual writers constantly warn us not to assume that we do nothing in solitude. To let go of our self-identity, we must have developed that self-identity until it is strong enough to submit to God. We must be willing to be simply who we are, under the eye of God. We must trust that such acceptance is not failure or weakness, but the means by which our soul will move ahead again.

The Philokalia[xxx] describes specific activities to be carried out in solitude:

  — constantly carry the prayer in our heart,
  — read the Psalms and other spiritual writings,

[xxx] Writings from the *Philokalia* on Prayer of the Heart, trans. E. Kadloubovsky and E.H. Palmer, 2nd ed. (London: Faber and Faber, 1954), pp. 57 and 219.

- think on Divine things, and
- work with our hands.

The writer also suggests that we not leave home or our place of solitude too often; and that we avoid meetings and conversations with anyone except in cases of direst need. Contact with others stimulates our senses and thereby hampers internal development.

Finally, we must focus our attention on the present and avoid letting our thoughts distract us.

In solitude we become comfortable with the silence of nothingness, the beingness of non-beingness. This solitude is being alive and alert, directed and intensely conscious. This solitude will lead to total silence.

Silence

Silence is the space where the mystery reveals itself. In silence we observe the hidden wonder, receive spiritual gifts, and lose the persistent awareness of our self. But silence is a special moment, not a state of being; and, like unification, it comes and goes. We can walk with a sense of union without being silent.

Silence, therefore, is extremely rare and we should not seek it as our only way of being. It is the room in which we perceive and conceive the precious treasures of the spiritual life. In silence our mind is free from forms, having no image of ourselves or anything else even for an instant. Within the wholeness of the Theocentric mind, created as a result of liberation from duality and illusion, our thought as we know it ceases.

Our mind does not become vacant; it is only empty of the familiar or self-reflecting. Our heart is free of fantasies and gives birth to Divine and mysterious ideas which play within. Finally, silence creates a vacuum where we recognize "newness," a new person, and the gifts of the Spirit.

The Gifts of the Spirit

At last we reach the gold at the end of the rainbow. Was the journey worth it; would we choose to do it again? No one can answer these questions before beginning, and once we experience the gifts of the Spirit, even in the faintest form, we can never turn back.

Our pain was the discomfort of the unknown and our refusal to give up.

Our fatigue and aridity created humility that still continues. The spiritual gifts derived from the practice of the prayer in the heart are

- profound joy,
- the presence of God with Its clarity and peace,
- light/illumination,
- Divine Love,
- communication with Spirit,
- freedom, and
- ultimate grace.

So, let's begin with profound joy.

PROFOUND JOY

This Joy is not the usual emotional joy; but a silent inner bliss that is steady and continual. It is an attitude, a state of mind, a way of being, that rests upon the experiences of a lifetime and penetrates our whole human being. Not casual or based on affirmations—this joy lives in every nook and cranny of our being, and rings and resounds and echoes in every portion of our soul.

It is the joy promised in Corinthians that "no eye has seen, nor ear heard, nor the heart of man conceived what God has prepared for those who love him."[xxxi] This joy comes from being totally connected inwardly to our spiritual being; it is a singing in the heart that can actually provide a physical sensation of love as has been my experience. It is a product of being so united with the prayer, that the prayer now "prays you," making your body, mind, and emotions vibrate like the harp string that sends forth overtones which last for several moments.

We are so united by the prayer, "all senses are occupied, so that none of them is free or able to act in any way, either outwardly or inwardly."[xxxii] We often feel such joy, in which our senses are lost, when we becomes enraptured with loving another person, or hearing a great musical work, seeing a beautiful painting, or immersed in our own creativity. Our mind, senses, and body are lost for a brief moment. With the Prayer of the Heart, the joy lasts longer, as the inner Presence is ever there in our awareness. This inner Presence is the cause of all other joys.

[xxxi] I Corinthians 2:9, Revised Standard Edition of the Bible.

[xxxii] St. Teresa of Avila, *The Life of Teresa of Jesus*, trans. E. Allison Peers (Garden City, NY: Image Books, 1960), p. 174.

This joy reflects the love we feel for the Divine, the product of our having loved God and connected everywhere with Him.

A FEELING OF THE PRESENCE OF GOD

Feeling God's Presence, we have no doubt that He is totally within and without. We are engulfed by Him. We feel carried, unself-possessed, and yet not afraid, knowing God is present. We know clarity and peace through this Presence.

If God is present, how can we have doubt or fear? Nothing can remove the feeling of the Presence as we move deeper and grow stronger in absolute faith.

The sense of incompleteness and dissatisfaction that troubled us before the spiritual fire was kindled in our hearts has ceased. The unrestrainable wanderings of thought from which we suffered have all ceased now. The atmosphere of the soul becomes clear and cloudless: there remains only one thought and only one remembrance, which is of God. There is clarity within and throughout, and in this clearness every movement is noticed and is valued according to its merits in the spiritual light that flows from the Lord whom we contemplate.[xxxiii]

LIGHT / ILLUMINATION

Our personality has been re-forming during this journey. This changed personality is present, but our interior has been so cleaned out that nothing can veil or separate our inner splendor, our Christ light, from shining. We embrace the light the mystics and saints so often refer to.

A "hollow" being is formed, but rather than being a frightening void, an empty tomb, it becomes a light-filled presence. We stand whole and strong, flexible and tender, free enough of ego defenses and definitions to create a holy, porous texture through which the light may shine. This light grows and springs up like a flame through the power of our attention, giving us a sense of total illumination.

DIVINE LOVE

Divine Love is the most powerful feeling

[xxxiii] *The Art of Prayer*, ed. Chariton of Valamo, trans. E. Kadloubovsky and E.M. Palmer, (London: Faber and Faber, 1956), p. 155.

available to anyone. We are in the midst of a Love without conscious involvement. It is inaccurate to equate this experience with a human sensation of love. Divine Love clearly transcends the human vehicle and is the overflow from a soul deeply connected with the internalized Spirit.

This Divine Love quickens our thoughts ever more directly toward God and dissipates our awareness of outer conditions.

COMMUNICATION WITH SPIRIT

People who practice the Prayer of the Heart and direct their lives toward immersion in the Spirit do talk with God. Others have questioned the sanity of those who make such admissions. Yet many seekers have acknowledged an inner Wisdom, which guides them in understanding the Divine mysteries God reveals in the silent depths of the heart. This awareness is always present, but dormant in the depths of our being, awaiting our contact. That contact occurs when we become silent and functioning only as the observer.

FREEDOM

Our destination is freedom:

- a free mind,
- a free heart,
- a free soul,
- free expression.

However, we can only acquire the spiritual gift of freedom after we have trained well, run the course, won and lost, learned the rules, and then through commitment moved beyond the physical and mental limits and entered the domain of unification with the Divine. After years of practice we find ourselves suddenly praying without thought. Then we know freedom.

In that moment our personality, mind and emotions are gone, and something else takes over. So it is in the Prayer of the Heart. The Prayer of the Heart distinguishes itself from other freedoms in that it leaves us open to all of life. As St. John describes it:

Oh, how happy a chance is this for the soul which can free itself... None can understand it, unless, as it seems to me, it be the soul that has experienced it. For such a soul will see clearly...the servitude in which it lay and (the) many miseries it was subject to when it was at the mercy of its faculties and desires, and will know how the life of the spirit is true liberty and wealth, bringing with it inestimable blessings.[xxxiv]

Ultimate Grace

Grace is the condition in which we express freedom, even though its presence does not mean life becomes easy. What has been gained then?

Life continues to provide occasions for learning; however, we are able to look at them in a new way; we are transformed.

Whatever our role in the world, we remain in the quiet, resting in the Presence. Doubt and discomfort may continue to come and go, but they do not tarnish our awareness of the Presence of God. Having this gift of grace is the sweetest way to live and to share while sojourning on earth.

[xxxiv] Saint John of the Cross, *The Dark Night of the Soul*, trans. E. Allison Peers, 3rd ed. (New York: Image Books, 1959), pp. 148-149.

ABOUT THE AUTHOR

When Carol Ruth Knox arrived as the minister at Unity of Walnut Creek, California in November 1970, she brought a unique perspective to which people quickly responded. Although Unity is basically a Christian movement, Carol Ruth incorporated teachings from all the major religions. She believed God speaks in every language and to every individual, not as an aloof, strict, punishing parent, who lives in a faraway place called Heaven. Rather, God lives as an indwelling presence to guide each of us to our highest calling.

On Sunday mornings she talked of an omnipresent God that she saw in everyone she met, even those most of us dismiss as demented. She saw God in every animal she encountered, every flower, tree and blade of grass. God was an active participant in her life, whether she behaved lovingly or reacted from anger. Each person, each animal, each interaction included God and had a lesson for her, a lesson that she shared with her congregation.

Carol Ruth taught that prayer is our way to connect with this God within. She studied extensively the lessons of the saints, especially Saints Theresa, Julian of Norwich, and John of the Cross. She studied to deepen her understanding of prayer's role in her daily life.

Her own Dark Night of the Soul led her to the Prayer of the Heart, which became the subject for her doctoral dissertation and the focus of her teachings. In numerous workshops around the country, she explained how we can transform our lives and reach a greater understanding of God by applying the simple, yet profound, practice of this prayer.

Although she died in 1987, her messages are timeless and still relevant today. I can attest to the wisdom and the Truth contained in this book.

- Coy F. Cross II, Editor, November 2015

About the Editor

As far back as I can remember, I have been seeking to know God. Growing up attending strict fundamentalist churches, I often felt confused by the inconsistent answers to my many questions and guilty, not only for what I did, but for the "worldly" thoughts that passed through my head. As a teenager I gave up hope of ever becoming as perfect as Jesus, which was my standard, and so I left the church.

I spent nearly 25 years as a self-described "antagonistic agnostic," ready with a sharp retort to anyone who tried to talk to me about God. As I approached 40, a feeling of something missing grew into a powerful yearning within me and I began to search for an answer.

After unsuccessfully exploring familiar church teachings, I visited a Unity Church on a friend's recommendation. I had difficulty at first because the positive message seemed so foreign to me. In October 1980, Carol Ruth Knox came as the guest speaker. Immediately I knew my search was over. This was the message I had been looking for. God was not a vengeful, human-like being, who expected me to be perfect; but an internal presence that constantly guided me to be my best self. During her talk, she and I made contact and there was an instant sense of recognition. We both knew we would be important in each other's life.

Within a few months, I moved to Walnut Creek and became a member of Carol Ruth's church and eventually served on the board of directors. She and I became dear friends, often having dinner or attending baseball games together. She became my minister, my teacher, my mentor, as well as my friend. Her ability to explain complex ideas in a language I could understand changed my view of God, the world, and my role in that world. I had found my spiritual home.

After her transition in 1987, I vowed to do all I could to preserve Carol Ruth's teachings and make them available for others. I am eternally grateful to have had the privilege of knowing this incredible teacher and having her as my friend. *The Prayer of the Heart* is another step in fulfilling my promise.

ENGAGE WITH COY F. CROSS II

Coy Cross II on Facebook

https://www.facebook.com/CoyFCrossIIPhd

Coy Cross II on YouTube

http://www.youtube.com/channel/UCfb8JPMD9P4
6pQHLmE1uN0Q

Coy Cross on the Web

Search "Coy F Cross" for interviews and more.

Coy Cross II on Twitter

https://twitter.com/coy_ii

Carol Ruth Knox and Coy F. Cross II

For more information about Carol Ruth Knox and her pioneering spiritual work visit:

http://CarolRuthKnox.com

https://www.facebook.com/RevCarolRuthKnoxPhd

Or order these books:

Coy Cross II in Print

"The Dhance: A Caregiver's Search for Meaning" by Coy F. Cross II, Ph.D. - practical spiritual help for a crisis

Buy it now!
http://carolruthknox.com/#TheDhance

Coy F. Cross II PhD

A Message from Coy F. Cross II, Author, about The Dhance: In 2009, my precious wife Carol Martha and I were told she had Stage 3, Level C ovarian cancer. These past three years [2009-2012] have been my 'graduate course' in deepening my relationship with both Carol Martha and the Divine.

I have come to know that God is right here, right now, in the midst of this terrible disease called cancer.

Testimonials

This book is a story of life at its best in the worst of experiences in the human journey. It gives us hope that we can always grow and discover who we truly are and what is important in life. A love story filled with life skills. — Rev. Beth Ann Suggs, PCC; Unity Minister

More than a powerful love story, <u>The Dhance</u> serves as a Spiritual Practice guide to courageously working through a major life crisis. —Greg Finch, Licensed Teacher, Unity Worldwide Ministries

Unity of Walnut Creek

http://www.unityofwalnutcreek.com/

A supportive spiritual community; Prayer support, Spiritual growth; Classes and workshops; Making a difference

A Detailed History of Carol Ruth Knox at Unity of Walnut Creek

http://data.unityofwalnutcreek.com/information/history_of_unity_01.pdf

Unity of Walnut Creek Historical Timeline

http://www.unityofwalnutcreek.com/walnut-creek-timeline

The main idea of the book is: The Western tendency to honor the individual is significant and important, but we must let go of our individuality to become a part of a community—the entire human race—connected to everything—a humble action full of nobility and dignity. The Prayer teaches the necessity of full self-identity before we can attain the state of humility. And once our personality is ready, all the Prayer asks is humility before God's Will always.